JESUS AND THE
BICAMERAL BRAIN

Knowing and Being

T0273571

JESUS AND THE
BICAMERAL BRAIN

Knowing and Being

James P. Danaher

Paragon House

First Edition 2021
Published in the United States by
Paragon House
Saint Paul, Minnesota

www.ParagonHouse.com

Bible references from the New Revised Standard Version unless otherwise noted.

Library of Congress Cataloging-in-Publication Data

Names: Danaher, James P., author.
Title: Jesus and the bicameral brain : knowing and being / James P.
   Danaher.
Description: First edition. | Saint Paul, Minnesota : Paragon House, 2021.
   | Includes bibliographical references. | Summary: "The bicameral brain
   gives us access to two different perspectives and levels of
   consciousness. The one perspective and level of consciousness gives us
   access to the world and what we need to know to be in the world, while
   the other gives us access to God and his creation. The gospel as
   something to simply know and believe is very different from the gospel
   as someone to be. The one is epistemic and is simply a doctrine to
   believe, the other a spiritual journey that creates the nature and
   character of our eternal being. This is not the popular gospel but it is
   the gospel that runs throughout the history of Christianity for those
   who take Jesus' words seriously"-- Provided by publisher.
Identifiers: LCCN 2021015030 (print) | LCCN 2021015031 (ebook) | ISBN
   9781557789471 (paperback) | ISBN 9781610831284 (ebook)
Subjects: LCSH: Jesus Christ--Knowableness. | Jesus Christ--Words. |
   Knowledge, Theory of (Religion) | Consciousness--Religious
   aspects--Christianity. | Faith and reason--Christianity.
Classification: LCC BT205 .D27 2021 (print) | LCC BT205 (ebook) | DDC
   231/.042--dc23
LC record available at https://lccn.loc.gov/2021015030
LC ebook record available at https://lccn.loc.gov/2021015031

Manufactured in the United States of America
10 9 8 7 6 5 4 3 2 1

This book is dedicated to the memory of my mother, Caroline Von Atzingen Danaher Janus or Nanny (1908-2003). She was my first experience of God's unconditional love from a human being. She gave me life in this world, and then at the end of her life, she blessed me through her Alzheimer's disease, and the way it brought me into the deeper life of which Jesus speaks, as I was blessed to care for her.

Acknowledgment

I would like to acknowledge and offer special thanks to my editor, Dorian Alu, for keeping me on track and making this work much more readable than it would have been without her. Also, I would like to thank Dr. Gordon Anderson, the publisher at Paragon House, who has given me a place from which to share my spiritual journey into the deeper life of the Gospels. Lastly, I would like to thank those former students, who are too many to list, for they have been God's instruments that have encouraged me to stay on the journey into the fullness of life to which Jesus call us.

Contents

Preface

We now know that the two hemispheres of the human brain function very differently, yet they work together in order to produce the full range of human experience and knowledge. Of course, we are still at very early stages of trying to understand how these two hemispheres of the brain interact with human consciousness; but what our present understanding has revealed is that while the left hemisphere of the brain specializes in organizing our experience into language and knowledge, the right hemisphere specializes in our broader experiences that often extend beyond our knowing. Certainly, there is some knowing that goes on in the right-brain and some raw experiences to which the left-brain has access, but for the most part, our knowing and those experiences that extend beyond our knowing seem to take place in different hemispheres of the brain.

Interestingly, the twentieth century has also brought us to understand truth in two very different ways as well. Epistemic truth is the truth of what we know, and is perhaps best understood with Aristotle's claim that human beings are involved in the three basic activities of making, doing, and knowing. When we make, we want to make what is beautiful; when we do, we want to do what is good; and when we know, we want to know what is true. Thus, epistemic truth is the truth of what we know. Ontological truth, on the other hand, is the truth of our being or the truth of who we are as a human being, which is much more mysterious and involves what we personally pursue as good and beautiful.

When Jesus says, "I am the way, and the truth, and the life,"[1] he is speaking of a truth that is something to be because it is ultimately good and divinely beautiful and not merely something to know because it is true. In terms of religious truth, however, most people prefer a truth that is merely something to know and believe. If the gospel is simply something to know and believe as true, that leaves us free to determine what is beautiful and good on our own. Our socio-cultural world has a lot to say about what is beautiful and good, but the concepts of beauty and goodness that we inherit from our socio-cultural world are almost always at odds with what Jesus has to say about such things. Jesus' words represent the meaning of life and the ultimate beauty and goodness of our being. Jesus' words are nothing like the doctrines and theologies that the popular religions endorse and propagate. His words are living words that are meant to take root at the core of our being and make us into Jesus' likeness, rather than the likeness of the world. As such, his words make little sense from our inherited, socio-cultural perspective in the world. His words are heavenly words and can only be heard from the perspective of who we are in God rather than from the perspective of who we are in the world.

Prayer, as Jesus understood it, is what puts us in contact with that different level of consciousness that allows us to experience the divine beauty and goodness of Jesus' words. That level of consciousness is very different from the level of consciousness through which we experience and understand the world, and we now seem to have evidence that it involves a different part of the

---

1. John 14:6.

brain as well. Our being in the world is directed primarily by the left-brain which contains almost all of the kind of knowledge essential to our being in the world. By contrast, the right-brain seems to give us access to experiences that transcend our knowing and speak to deeper levels of our being.

The claim of this book is that Jesus' words cannot be heard from the left-brain's understanding that we have inherited from the world. Thus, people who insist upon building their lives upon that understanding have to create a version of Christianity that avoids the words of Jesus. Christians claim to love Jesus, but most hate the things he says. Thus, the popular gospel offers us doctrines that by-pass his words and offer us a Jesus that is more appealing to who we are in the world. The popular Christian doctrines of our day appeal to the same mind and level of consciousness that connects us to the world, but the words of Jesus are speaking to that level of consciousness that connects us to God rather than the world. Doctrines and theologies are epistemic truths that are things to know and believe. The epistemic truths of religion and science are comforting because they are shared by many people, which give such beliefs the appearance of truth. Jesus' words, however, represent the ontological truth of our being, and are shared by very few. The epistemic truths in which we place our trust can be acquired in an instant. The ontological truth of the kind of being to which Jesus calls us is acquired through a spiritual journey whereby we are made evermore into Jesus' likeness as more and more of Jesus' words take root at the core of our being. This is the deeper life to which Jesus calls us, and it always comes with the question: how far do you want to go with Jesus?

CHAPTER ONE

The Bicameral Brain

Jill Taylor was a thirty-seven year old brain anatomist teaching at the Harvard Medical School. One morning in 1996, as she was showering, she began to have strange experiences. Because of the nature of the experiences and her understanding of the brain, she realized she was having a massive stroke in the left hemisphere of her brain. As a brain anatomist, she knew exactly where the stroke was taking place, and she also knew that if she didn't get help she would die. As the left-brain was cutting out, however, the right-brain started to kick in, and she began having such mystical experiences that she almost didn't care whether she lived or died. She did manage to survive the stroke and most of her book, *My Stroke of Insight* is about her recovery, which took several years, but she was eventually able to recover all of the faculties that the stroke initially seemed to destroy.[2]

We have known of the bicameral nature of the human brain since the time of the Greeks. What we did not know until recently was how the two hemispheres of the human brain functioned. Today, advances in technology have allowed us to discover much more than we have ever known about the different functions of the

---

2. Taylor, Jill. *My Stroke of Insight: A Brain Scientist's Personal Journey.* Penguin Books, 2009.

human brain and its two asymmetrical hemispheres. Early research into these two hemispheres of the brain initially led us to believe that the two hemispheres behaved somewhat independently of one another and provided us with the very different functions that constitute our human experience. More recent research reveals the matter to be more complex. Iain McGilchrist's, *The Master and His Emissary: The Divided Brain and the Making of the Western World*, does an enormously comprehensive job of showing how the two hemispheres work together, but also represent two very different ways of both understanding and experiencing the world. Both hemispheres of the brain are involved in every part of our experience including: language, emotions, reason, and creativity. What distinguishes one hemisphere from the other according to McGilchrist is the matter of attention and how our attention is focused.

McGilchrist points out that birds and mammals, as well as human beings, have bicameral brains. In fact, in birds that have their eyes on different sides of their heads, the left eye connects to the right hemisphere and right eye to the left hemisphere, giving them the ability to understand their environment in two very different ways. The right eye, and its connection to the left hemisphere, gives the bird the ability to narrowly focus on food sources in order to detect the difference between a pebble and an edible seed. Survival, however, also requires the bird's ability to focus upon the larger horizon in order to detect and avoid predators that would make the bird their own food source.

These different functions of the bicameral brain are also represented in the human brain, although in human beings the left-brain specializes in acquiring language and all of the knowledge associated with language in order for us to survive and prosper in the world. The left-brain specializes in creating language that analytically distinguishes one thing from another, while the right-brain is able to see connections between things that are often more difficult to express in concrete terms, and therefore its use of language is often more metaphorical. The right-brain even seems to be open to experiences that transcend language completely, and silence seems to be the only word that comes close to express the experience of simply being connected to other beings and being itself. Since a great deal of what we need to know in order to survive and prosper in the world comes to us as a cultural inheritance, language is the basis for acquiring that understanding of the world. As a culture becomes more complex, language and the left-brain becomes more important, and experiences that could not be reduced to words comes to be seen as less meaningful concerning our survival and prosperity in the world.

By contrast, however, the right-brain does seem to give us access to experiences that extend beyond what we can know and express with words. Many aesthetic, moral, or spiritual experiences are too intimate for words. They are the deeper experiences to which the right-brain seems to give us access. Because modern culture has been dominated by the kind of understanding that the left-brain has inherited from the world; that understanding is quick to filter out any right-brain experiences that do not conform to the understanding the left-brain has inherited from the world. If, however, we are able to resist the left-brain's mastery over those deeper experiences, we are able to experience a God that is beyond our knowing but not beyond our experience. This is the pure awareness that cannot be reduced to knowing. It is the experience of God before that experience can be translated into an idol that makes sense to the understanding we have inherited from the world.

Our left-brain, which attaches us to the world and what we need to know for our survival and prosperity in the world, is the knowing mind that constantly floods us with data concerning the world and our place in it. The right-brain, however, is able to go beyond our knowing and experience the pure awareness of consciousness itself. The left-brain specializes in paying attention to the data that the world presents us with in order for us to make judgments about that data, while the right-brain is capable of the pure awareness that makes no judgment and considers no data. Awareness that does not rush to judgment is a different level of consciousness that is not like thinking or knowing. If our thinking and knowing are over-developed, we become dominantly left-brained and we find pure awareness very difficult, but the pure awareness that does not rush to judgment is what has allowed for the evolution of our species, as well as our own individual spiritual evolution. Without an awareness that is disconnected from the world, we are trapped in the knowing and thinking we inherit from our particular time and place in human history.

It is the world that tells us how to understand the objects we encounter in life, but we are also capable of raw experiences or awareness that transcends the knowing we inherit from the world. According to McGilchrist, the transcendent awareness of the right-brain is the master to the emissary that is our left-brain and all of its knowing. Pure awareness is what opens us to what is beyond our knowing. It is the larger mind that connects us to something bigger than ourselves and our understanding. It is not the thinking mind but an awareness of being itself that transcends our thinking and understanding, but not our experience.

Unfortunately, in our modern Western world the left-brain has become so dominant that many consider the broader experiences of the right-brain meaningless by comparison. The major claim of McGilchrist's book is to challenge that notion and argue that the left-brain, which houses most of our knowledge concerning our being in the world, is the mere emissary of the right-brain. His claim is that while the left-brain appears to know how to negotiate our existence in the world, it does not have access to the larger spectrum of our experience as does its master the right-brain. Emissaries can often think of themselves as the essential agent that gets things done, but emissaries do not see the larger picture to which the master, and not the emissary, has access. McGilchrist's claim is that Western Civilization has elevated the emissary or left-brain to a place of dominance in spite of the fact that it does not have access to the broader experiences of the right-brain.

Although the kind of knowing we associate with language is largely a left-brain activity, it lacks the larger perspective that gives us access to the imagination and experiences that transcend the kind of knowing we inherit from the world through language. As children, we initially acquire language, and the early knowledge associated with language, uncritical as an inheritance from our particular time and place in human history. For many people, the understanding that the left-brained acquired in childhood lasts a lifetime, and data that contradict that understanding is simply dismissed. Of course, if everyone were dominantly left-brained, there would be no human history, since change only comes about by our ability to recognize anomalies to our inherited understanding.

The left-brain is great at acquiring knowledge but the right-brain seems to have access to anomalous data that allows us to challenge what we know in order to create better perspectives and understandings. The more open we are to our broader right-brain experiences and the anomalies they provide, the more open we are to changing our minds about what we claim to know. People with excessive security needs will tend to avoid the anomalous data and cling to what they purport to know. Indeed, the right-brain and the experiences to which it gives us access can be unsettling, since they are personal and not the kind of common understanding we share with others from our cultural tribe and language community. Of course, if we over identify with the right-brain and its anomalous experiences, we can be deemed crazy, an oddball, a genius, or a saint. People who tend to identify with the right-brain and the kinds of experiences to which it gives us access are the deviants who are often persecuted because they represent a threat to the status quo. Such people, however, are also the individuals who move human history forward, not through what they know, but through the broader and often unsettling experiences to which the right-brain gives us access. This is McGilchrist's ultimate claim, and I believe he is right. We have the capacity to see beyond what we have been told to see, but we have to exercise that freedom and assume its risk. This is faith in its ultimate form; it is the belief that there is more meaning to life than we have been told, and faith in our right-brain experiences allows us to explore that deeper meaning. Knowledge is something we share with others, faith is a personal journey whereby we leave the safe harbor of what we claim to know and explore the deeper mystery of who we really are.

Of course, the purpose of this book is not to link different forms of thinking or levels of consciousness to different hemispheres of the brain. To begin with, we know almost nothing of the connection between physical activity in the brain and human consciousness. What is interesting, however, is that our recent discoveries concerning the different functions of the bicameral brain are not that new, or at least one aspect of them is not that new. Indeed, premodern, medieval thinkers understood the difference between the kind of knowledge we associate with language and share with others, and the kind of experiences that transcend language and knowledge.

Without understanding how the bicameral brain functioned, the medieval idea of these two very different faculties of human experience and knowledge were divided between the apophatic and kataphatic. The apophatic, or not knowing, were those experiences that could not be reduced to the kind of knowing that can be represented with language, while the kataphatic was knowledge that could be made common and shared through language. The advance of human knowledge happens through the apophatic or what McGilchrist claims are right-brain activities that transcend what we purport to know. Our broader experiences are what prompt our imagination to conceptualize the world anew in order to account for anomalous experiences that extend beyond, and are not compatible with, what we commonly claim to know. Certainly, we can, and many people do, simply avoid those anomalous experiences and cling to the initial understanding we received through language and the conceptualization of the world that language provides. The spiritual and intellectual journey that has created human history, however, is always led by the apophatic rather than what we purport to know. Human history advances because we are able to experience anomalies to our inherited understanding that force us to conceptualize the world anew.

At the end of the sixteenth and beginning of the seventeenth centuries the inventions of the microscope and telescope revealed more about the world than Aristotle could have ever imagined. Such additional data brought about the transition from an Aristotelian understanding of physics to a Newtonian understanding, and the transition from a geocentric universe to a heliocentric universe. The transition to a new way of conceptualizing the world is usually slow and met with resistance. If the new data is unsettling to some of our deeply held beliefs and values, the resistance will be enormous and can take centuries. It took generations for Newton to replace Aristotle, and that was just a matter of adapting to the anomalies that the microscope provided. If the anomalous experiences represent a serious threat to our inherited beliefs and values, it can take much longer. The greatest and most obvious examples of this are the words of Jesus.

Jesus' words tell us to love our enemies and not to respond to violence with violence, but just suffer the violence without responding in kind.[3] Jesus' words tell us to judge no one,[4] and forgive everyone or God will not forgive us.[5] Christianity is the largest religion in the world, yet very few Christians take Jesus' words

---

3. Matthew 5:38-45.
4. Matthew 7:1-2.
5. Matthew 6:15, and Mark 11:26.

seriously. They are simply too anomalous to our inherited understanding, so we do with them what we do with any experiences that are too contrary to our inherited understanding – we ignore them. Jesus' words will always be filtered out by the inherited, cultural understanding of our left-brain. Indeed, they can only be heard from a different level of consciousness, which apparently involves a different part of our brain as well. This different level of consciousness seems to be what the medieval mystics understood as prayer. Prayer, as a different level of consciousness which allows us to experience the beauty and goodness of Jesus' words without them being filtered-out through our left-brain's inherited understanding of the world, is a very different notion of prayer than most have today.

It is not easy to experience such an alternative level of consciousness. Experiences that are contrary to the understanding into which we have been acculturated are not easily embraced. If you were white and born in the first half of the twentieth century in the American south, you were acculturated into a racist understanding of the world. That was probably true for a lot of people living in the north as well. The belief that people are racially different from one another was a common and popular belief at the time, and has not completely disappeared. If your experiences were contrary to that belief, you were forced to choose between the knowing you inherited from your culture, and your experiences which were contrary to that acculturation.

Going with experiences that are contrary to your acculturation always put you at odds with the world; and Jesus' words are always at odds with our acculturated understanding of the world, since they are heavenly words and always incompatible with the understanding we have inherited from the world. We can claim to know Jesus through our inherited understanding of the world, but such knowledge has to be through created doctrines and theologies that are compatible with the world, rather than the words of Jesus, since his words are almost always at odds with our inherited understanding. Jesus' words are not meant to fit neatly into our inherited left-brain's understanding of the world. His words are meant to undermine our inherited understanding and make us into something very different from the kind of being that our inherited understanding of the world has created. As such, his words are not things to know along with all the other things our left-brain knows, but are apophatic experiences that are purely personal and speak to a deeper level of consciousness than the level of consciousness that connects us to the world.

God has equipped us with such a level of consciousness that is able to experience an unknowable God. The creator of the universe is far beyond our knowing but not beyond our experience. We keep making up theologies and doctrines that attempt to reduce God to something knowable rather than something to experience on that deeper level of consciousness that transcends our knowing but not our experience. We are transformed by our experience rather than what we claim to know. Our knowledge keeps us anchored to our inherited understanding of the world, but there are levels of consciousness that can take us beyond what we claim to know.

The level of consciousness through which we know the world is not our only level of consciousness, nor is it our original level of consciousness. Before the world got a hold of us and began shaping us into its likeness, we had experiences that were very different from those experiences we would later have in the world. Our first experiences were those of being connected to and, indeed, engulfed within another being. In our initial state in the womb, and for a short time after our birth, we had experiences that were very different from those we would have after the world got a hold of us and taught us how to interpret our experiences as independent subjects surround by a world of objects. In our initial, unitive state of consciousness, we experienced being connected to another being and having everything provided for us by that other being. This initial state of consciousness was very different from the dualistic consciousness of the subject/object perspective that we later acquire from the world. Shortly after our birth, we began to experience a separation from the one to whom we were originally joined, and we begin to see ourselves as isolated subjects surrounded by a world of strange objects. This subject/object distinction became the new perspective through which we perceived and began to acquire our understanding of the world, but our initial level of unitive consciousness remained at least on the unconscious level. Since the science of the unconscious is only a little over one hundred years old, our exploration of this initial, unitive consciousness is at a very early stage.

Although this earliest level of unitive consciousness is not something to which we have easy access, and today is relegated to the unconscious level, it seems to be very similar to that level of consciousness which the medieval mystics referred to it as the apophatic or not knowing level of our experience. In a certain sense, Sigmund Freud (1856-1939) did not discover the unconscious; he redefined it in terms that were compatible with our modern thinking. Prior to the modern period, mystics had always explored the unconscious but understood it in a different context and used different terminology. This is not to say that Freud's idea of the unconscious and the mystics idea of the apophatic are the same thing. They certainly are not, but they are both exploring levels of consciousness that are very different from that knowing level of consciousness that connects us to the world.

A big difference between Freud and the mystics is that while Freud explores those deeper levels of consciousness through the subject/object perspective that we inherit from the world, the mystics explored those deeper levels of consciousness through our original unitive consciousness of being connected to another being and Being itself. The mystic's notion of prayer explores those deeper levels of consciousness through the experience of our unitive consciousness rather than through the subject/object perspective we have received from the world.

The bicameral nature of the human brain provides us with more than a single perspective, and we can perceive the world either as a world of objects distinct from ourselves as conscious subjects, or as a consciousness that is somehow connected to other conscious beings and to consciousness itself. Many people, especially in our modern world, seem to live almost exclusively out of the left-brain and all of its acculturated understanding of the objects that surround them. Others, however, explore the deeper experiences of unitive consciousness through prayer or mediation. For those who live exclusively out of their left-brain's acculturated understanding of the world, there is no deeper level of consciousness and God is yet another object to which our cultural tribe teaches us how to respond and manipulate in order to accomplish our purposes. Prior to that level of consciousness, however, there was the experience of being engulfed within another being. That is the level of unitive consciousness that mystics of nearly every tradition explore. It is also the only level of consciousness that is able to make sense of Jesus' words. When we are able to see our connection to consciousness itself, and all other conscious beings, the words of Jesus make sense in a way that they do not make sense when our only perspective is that of an isolated subject in a world of threatening objects. This ineffable reality of being *in* another Being is always there but we only become aware of it through that deeper level of unitive consciousness that we are able to experience in prayer or meditation. If we never go to that other level of consciousness, we can all too easily become amoral people without any sense of that unitive consciousness which links us to God and other human beings. If we live exclusively out of our left-brain's subject/object perspective, we can act morally for fear of appearing to be amoral and the consequences that would have upon our life in the world, but we will never be capable of loving "our neighbor as ourselves." To love our neighbor as ourselves requires that different level of unitive conscious that is very different from the subject/object perspective and level of consciousness that connects us to the world.

The left-brain's subject/object perspective is about the survival and prosperity of the individual, but without spending time in the kind of prayer that exercises our unitive consciousness, which gives us the inner experience of our connection to other conscious beings and Being itself, our morality is simply an act to enhance our status in the world. True morality comes out of a different level of consciousness where we recognize our neighbor, and even our enemy, as ourselves. This unitive consciousness that connects us to God and other human beings is nothing like the consciousness which connects us to the world. There are no words that can stand in for this experience of unitive consciousness, the way words stand in for our experience of objects. This deep experience of connectedness was perhaps the reason the ancient Jews refused to articulate the name of God, who cannot be reduced to names or words, but can be experienced on a deeper level of consciousness than that level with which we interact with the world.

According to research, language, and the kind of knowledge we associate with language, is predominantly a left-brain activity, but our experience is able to transcend the kind of knowledge we associate with language. The mystic experience of our connection to God and other human beings is not something that can be known in the same way we come to know the world through the subject/object perspective that we associate with the left-brain. The experience of our unitive consciousness is purely personal and must be a first-hand experience rather than the kind of second-hand knowing that can be expressed in words and shared with other human beings. Mystics have often explained this experience as the "reign of God" in which we participate, not as knowers, but as being part of God's being in the world. It is an inner rather than outer experience and usually accessed by turning off our connection to external objects and our thoughts concerning them.

As we have said, long before we had any understanding of the asymmetrical nature of the bicameral brain, the Greek terms used for these two very different human faculties of knowing and experiences that transcend our knowing were the kataphatic and apophatic. The left-brain seems more suited for kataphatic knowing, while the right-brain seems to give us access to apophatic experiences that are not reducible to language and the kind of knowing associated with language. Apophatic experience is quite literally a matter of not knowing, and the wisdom that come from not knowing, or not being able to tie down our knowing with words that make sense from the subject/object perspective. Whatever language we do use to express our experiences on this deeper level of unitive consciousness is usually metaphorical rather than literal.

As McGilchrist points out, that can all too easily make the kataphatic or left-brain look superior to the right-brain and its alternative level of consciousness, but, in fact, it is the "not knowing" of the right-brain that drives the advance of human knowledge and the evolution of our species. Again, this is why McGilchrist claims that the right-brain is the master, and the knowing left-brain the emissary. That, however, is not the common view of either our science or religion.

Kataphatic or left-brain knowledge seems to have been dominant throughout our Western history, at least since the time of Aristotle. It is our ability to reduce the world of our experience to something knowable. The way the left-brain does this is by dividing the world of our experience into objects that can be labelled with words and concepts that can eventually be made into theories, maps, or beliefs that make sense of our experience. This is not something we do for ourselves, however. It is an inheritance that we receive from the socio-cultural world into which we are born. Our early education is a matter of receiving the way past generations have organized and disseminated their experience into a cultural understanding that made sense from the perspective of a particular time and place in human history. That inherited understanding, however, was not the product of left-brained individuals who simply passed on an inherited understanding from one generation to another. Human history is created by individuals who experience anomalies to the common understanding they inherit, and they suggest ways to accommodate those anomalies by altering, or sometimes radically changing, the inherited understanding. That process of producing new ways to conceptualize and understand things comes out of that different level of consciousness that gives us access to the imagination and creativity. Individuals who exercise this other level of consciousness are generally not received well. True, if they limit their creative activities to art or music, they will be tolerated, but if they venture into science or religion they most often do not end well. History might laud them, but they are generally scorned as the heretics of their day, and only seen as heroic to future generations. Again, this is the reason McGilchrist claims that the left-brain is the *Emissary* of its *Master*: the right-brain.

I should mention, as McGilchrist does repeatedly, that the left and right hemispheres of the brain constantly work together in order to provide us with the full range of human experience. It is certainly not that all of knowing exists on one side of the brain and our experiences that transcend that knowing are on the other side of the brain, but that model or paradigm does give us a way to understand the difference between our knowledge and those experiences that extend beyond what we know. Like all models or paradigms, it does not reflect reality but gives us a better way to understand our human condition.

We have been placed inside of a great mystery, and we are constantly either trying to reduce that mystery to something knowable, or exploring better perspectives to understand the deeper meanings of the mystery. This is really what McGilchrist is speaking about with the bicameral brain. He is simply using the idea of the bicameral brain as a way of speaking about these two very different levels of dealing with this mystery in which we find ourselves. We can either accept the understanding the world provides, or we can explore the mystery in order to find ever deeper levels of meaning. That, rather than the technical differences between the two hemispheres of the brain, is the point that McGilchrist is ultimately trying to make, and the point that I am trying to make as well.

Perhaps the best way to understand the bicameral brain is in terms of the journey that appears to be the human condition. In childhood, we are acculturated into a certain understanding, which seems to be housed primarily in our left-brain. Our right-brain, however, is capable of experiences that are not compatible with our left-brain's inherited understanding. The question is do we side with our inherited understanding and dismiss anything contrary to it, or do we explore those experiences to which our deeper level of consciousness give us access.

The more we identify with the world and the understanding the world has given us, the more quickly and unconsciously we translate our experiences through the knowing of the left-brain. Thus, we eliminate data that does not conform to our understanding and we confirm data that does conform. Cognitive dissonance theory involves the idea that once our minds are made up, we eliminate data and experiences that conflict with that data, and confirmation bias is the idea that we confirm data that supports our beliefs. People who live exclusively out of the left-brain's inherited understanding find it very difficult to experience anything that would contradict that understanding. On the other hand, people who are open to levels of consciousness beyond the kataphatic level of knowing are capable of experiences that present anomalies to what we claim to know. Perhaps the best way to explain these right-brain experiences is with the word, *behold*. Beholding is an experience that seems out of sync with our left-brain's understanding, but it is so powerful that we cannot dismiss it.

In the Bible when God or an angelic being appears, the word often used is "behold". Behold means do not dismiss this experience because it does not conform to your understanding of the world. Nearly all of Jesus' commandments are meant to be "beheld" and dealt with through a different process than we deal with other data that does not conform to our understanding. Beholding is the mystic experience of something that does not conform to our understanding, but is, nevertheless, compelling and captures our attention. Jesus' words are meant to be beheld rather than simply dismissed because they do not conform to our inherited understanding of the world. Indeed, it is hard to find any words of Jesus that are compatible with the left-brain understanding that we have inherited from the world.

Jesus' understanding of God is nothing like the understanding of God that we inherit from the world. Our inherited understanding of God is from the subject/object perspective. From that perspective, God is a distant sovereign who desires worship and obedience. Jesus' concept of God is that of a loving Father who desires that we would be made into the likeness of our heavenly Father. God as a sovereign law giver, who seeks obedience and punishes disobedience, may resemble some of our fathers, but if we pay attention to Jesus' words, we see that is not the kind of Father that Jesus understands God to be. The best of fathers desire their children to be like themselves in terms of character and virtue. Unfortunately, when Jesus reveals what that divine character and virtue look like, it is nothing like the kind of character and virtue that the world tells us to pursue in order to enhance our life in the world. From our perspective in the world, Jesus' words have little value. Of course, his words were never meant to appeal to who we are in the world, and neither can his words take root in the person we are in the world. They require the deep soil of our soul or who we were in God before the world got a hold of us and began making us in its likeness rather than the likeness of our heavenly Father. In order to make sense of Jesus' words, they need to be beheld by that unitive consciousness that we had before the world got a hold of us.

From the dualistic mind of the left-brain, and its subject/object perspective, God is yet another object that we have to learn to manipulate and control through our worship, right beliefs, and behavior. Jesus, however, tells us that God is "our Father" whose only desire is that we would become ever more like our Father rather than the world. Knowing your Father is personal and nothing like the kind of knowing that the world tells us is important.

Personal knowing is a radically different understanding than the understanding we have inherited from the world. Knowing God through the subject/object perspective of the left-brain is common and the basis for religious doctrines and theologies. In order to create such a common understanding, the left-brain has to eliminate data that cannot be reduced to a common understanding. McGilchrist often refers to this knowledge that the left-brain creates with the metaphor of maps, because what maps do is they eliminate all the particular data that is not relative to accomplishing a particular task, like getting from New York to Chicago. That is also what theories and principles do as well; they give us guidelines that we can all share to accomplish particular tasks. Thus, we create the idea of objective reality, or reality that appears to be more substantial than our own individual experiences, especially our internal experiences, because it is a reality that is shared by a great many people. What the left-brain produces, however, is not objective reality at all, but an abstraction that is very different from what we actually experience. Still, because it is shared by a great number of people, it can easily be mistaken for being more real than the actual experience of individuals. In the modern period this idea of objective reality became dominant through the advance of both modern science and modern religion.

At the beginning of the modern era, the invention of the microscope brought about the corpuscular philosophy, which eventually evolved into atomic chemistry. Adherents to this new way of thinking included such notables as Galileo Galilei (1564-1642), Rene Descartes (1596-1650), John Locke (1632-1704), and Isaac Newton (1643-1727), just to mention a few. The problem that the microscope produced was the fact that it allowed us to observe things that had never been observed before and therefore there was no inherited nomenclature for what was being experienced. Because the microscope revealed stuff that no one had ever experienced, the early corpuscularians had to create an understanding of what they were observing without the help of any inherited understanding. What they eventually settled on was the distinction between primary and secondary qualities: primary qualities being what was in the object itself independent of our experience of it, and secondary qualities being what was in us as observers rather than the objects themselves. The primary qualities that most agreed upon were extension, shape, number, motion and rest; while the secondary qualities were things like color, taste, sound, and smell, which were thought to be qualities that were in us rather than the object itself. Obviously, things like color, taste, sound, and smell are relative to the particular sensory faculties of our species, and part of our observation of things rather than the way things are in themselves independent of our observation of them. Of course, the same thing could be said for primary qualities, although perhaps to a lesser extent. That lesser extent, however, seemed to be enough to establish the idea of objective reality, or reality stripped of the biases that our particular perspective provides. Later generations would point out the fallacy of objective reality, but the value of the maps and theories that modern science was able to produce seemed to have valuable consequences that were hard to deny. Unfortunately, it also gave many people the idea that objective reality was real and not merely an abstract idea created for the purpose of making useful maps and theories. A road map for a trip from New York to Chicago certainly eliminates our personal biases, and it is a useful tool, but it hardly represents objective reality. The maps or theories of modern science are abstractions and nothing like the reality of what we actually experience, but since they can be commonly agreed upon by a great number of people, they appear more substantial than our actual experience.

A similar thing occurred in the religious thinking of the modern period as well. The medieval mystics spoke of beautifully divine internal experiences, but what would dominate so much of modern Christianity was the idea of the objective truth of the gospel. By analogy to the corpuscular philosophy and atomic chemistry, the way the experience of God's presence and Jesus' words affect us are like the secondary qualities of the corpuscular philosophy; but what was seen as the objective or essential truth of the gospel, was what was independent of our individual experiences and was shared as an objective truth. That objective truth, however, was in fact an abstraction, like a road map between New York and Chicago, although in the case of modern Christianity it became a road map to heaven. Thus, much of modern Christianity became a matter of our left-brain's knowing, rather than the transformative, personal experiences of our unitive consciousness.

Although, our modern science and religion have suppressed right-brain levels of consciousness and privileged the left-brain, there is a long history of right-brain cognition, both east and west. True, it is more routinely associated with eastern thinking, but it is also apparent among the Greek pre-Socratic philosophers, as well as the Christian mystics from the desert fathers and mothers to the great Spanish mystics of the sixteenth century. Additionally, the Jewish Kabbalah and Muslim Sufis also represent the kind of cognition that goes beyond our normal notions of knowing.

Of course, we live in a culture that has favored the left-brain and the sense of security that come from our trust in what we claim to know, but there does seem to be increased interest in the kind of *apophatic*, right-brain experiences so beautifully described by the Desert Fathers and Mothers and the medieval Christian Mystics. The twentieth century seems to have witnessed a rebirth of this apophatic, mystic tradition initially through the work of Thomas Merton (1915-1968) and more recently the work of Thomas Keating (1923-2018). Keating refers to this apophatic experience as centering prayer, which focuses upon consciousness itself rather than allowing our consciousness to focus upon any particular object the way our minds are so apt to do. When our consciousness is free from all objects of thought, the thinking subject is lost as well, since the subject/object perspective is eliminated once one side of the dichotomy is lost. The idea of subject and object are relative terms like up and down or inside and outside; if *up* is not relevant to what we are talking about, neither is *down*. Likewise, if there are no objects upon which to focus our attention, ourselves as observing subjects loses its meaning as well; and our experience is from a different perspective than the subject/object perspective of the left-brain. Thus, the mystic's practice of prayer attempts to return us to that initial, unitive state of consciousness where we were part of another being that provided all that we needed.

The apophatic experience of prayer is the practice of resting in our original state of unitive consciousness, where we are in God and God is in us. This original level of unitive consciousness appears to be very different from that level of consciousness that is aware of our being in the world. The world constantly demands our attention, but there is a level of consciousness that refuses the world's demands and allows us to experience pure awareness, which connects us to God and all other human beings. This is not a level of consciousness that is easily achieved, and it must be practiced, but when it is achieved, it provides us with a sense of being one with the experience itself, rather than as an observer who claims to know the experience as an object apart from itself. This is the unitive experience of being connected to God and

God's creation. It is this unitive experience that allowed Catherine of Genoa (1447-1510) to say, "My deepest me is God." Likewise, it is what Jesus is trying to teach us when he says, "The Father and I are one."[6]

The religious leaders of Jesus' day called this blasphemy and put Jesus to death because of it. Followers of Jesus eventually made his claim to be one with the Father into the doctrine of the trinity and tried to explain it through left-brain analysis, but it is not something to be *known* but something to be *experienced*. The experience of being one with God and different from God at the same time is the effect of our bicameral brain and not a metaphysical puzzle to be solved. The bicameral brain equips us with the ability to experience both a world that we can claim to know, and a God that appears unknowable but renders experiences so beautiful and good that they exceed our knowing, but not our experience. If we practice this apophatic prayer enough that we come to identify with its level of unitive consciousness, rather than who we are in the world, we will eventually be able to *behold* the words of Jesus and prevent them from being filtered out by the understanding we have inherited from the world.

Such a level of consciousness, however, can and usually does put us at odds with the world. Right-brain experiences of deeper levels of consciousness capable of revealing the beauty and goodness of Jesus' words do not conform to the maps and theories that the world sets before us. The broader, right-brain experiences that are unique to individuals are generally not appreciated by people who strongly identify with their left-brain's maps and theories.

---

6. John 10:30.

Heretics have always represented a threat to the security that most people derive from believing what everyone else believes, but the truth of what we have been taught to believe is very different from the authentic and ontological truth to which Jesus calls us.

The words of Jesus do not have an objective meaning the way doctrines do. Jesus' words are living words meant to take root at the core of our being in order to make us into his likeness. We may begin the spiritual journey to which Jesus calls us from the subject/object perspective that the world has given us, and from that perspective, God is the ultimate object that must be feared, obeyed, and worshiped. If we progress in the spiritual journey, however, and get to a place from which we can receive Jesus' word that God is "our Father", we begin to experience God in an entirely different way. In order to get us to that deeper level of experiencing God, Jesus has to destroy, or at least unsettle, what we claim to know about God. For example, Jesus says,

> Do not think that I have come to abolish the law or the prophets; I have come not to abolish but to fulfill. For truly I tell you, until heaven and earth pass away, not one letter, not one stroke of a letter, will pass from the law until all is accomplished. Therefore, whoever breaks one of the least of these commandments, and teaches others to do the same, will be called least in the kingdom of heaven; but whoever does them and teaches them will be called great in the kingdom of heaven. For I tell you, unless your righteousness exceeds that of the scribes and Pharisees, you will never enter the kingdom of heaven.[7]

---

7. Matthew 5:17-20.

Having said this, Jesus then gives six examples of what the law had said, and what he says in contradiction to the law. The law said, you shall not murder, but Jesus says do not be angry with your brother or sister.[8] The law said, you shall not commit adultery, but Jesus says that lust is equivalent to adultery.[9] The law said, a man could divorce his wife and remarry, but Jesus equates that with adultery.[10] The law said that we were to keep our oaths, but Jesus says to pledge no oath.[11] The law said, "An eye for an eye and a tooth for a tooth,"[12] but Jesus says, "If anyone strikes you on the right cheek, turn the other also."[13] Finally, Jesus says,

> You have heard that it was said, 'You shall love your neigh-
> bor and hate your enemy.' But I say to you, Love your ene-
> mies and pray for those who persecute you, so that you may
> be children of your Father in heaven.[14]

Jesus' words are not calling us to obedience to laws, but to the fulfillment of the law. A loving Father gives laws not in order to make his daughters and sons obedient but to make them like their Father in terms of character and virtue. This is the fulfillment of the law.

According to Jesus, God is not a distant sovereign who demands obedience and punishes disobedience, but a loving

---

8. Matthew 5:22.
9. Matthew 5:28.
10. Matthew 5:32.
11. Matthew 5:34-37.
12. Matthew 5:38.
13. Matthew 5:39.
14. Matthew 5:43-44.

Father who desires to make his daughters and sons into his forgiving and merciful likeness for having received forgiveness and mercy at ever greater depths. This is the ultimate fulfillment of the law that Jesus reveals. How far we want to follow Jesus into the depths of God's love is what the spiritual journey and repentance or changing our mind is all about. The righteousness of which Jesus speaks is not the righteousness of keeping the law, or having our sins forgiven, but the righteousness of becoming God's forgiveness, mercy, and love to the world. This is the fulfillment of the law that Jesus' words reveal.

As children, we might have imagined that the law our parents laid down was meant to make us obedient. In time, however, if we had good parents, we realize that what they commanded us to do was not to simply make us obedient but to make us into their likeness in terms of character and virtue. Of course, we only come to that understanding with maturity, and spiritual maturity only comes by staying on the journey and allowing Jesus' words to become our own. The law was never intended to make us righteous in the sense of being obedient, although that is where we usually begin the spiritual journey. Jesus' words reveal our need for forgiveness and mercy on ever deeper levels in order that we might love much for having been forgiven much, since "the one to whom little is forgiven, loves little."[15] The thing that keeps us from being forgiven much is the idea that being forgiven makes us righteous. But Jesus' idea of righteousness is not that our sins have been forgiven, but that we would become his forgiveness and mercy to the world.

---

15. Luke 7:47.

CHAPTER TWO

Epistemic and Ontological Truth

Knowing who is in and who is out with God seems like a very valuable piece of information, but it is the very thing that prevents us from hearing the words of Jesus, which always have to be heard from a place of not knowing. There is a big difference between the epistemic truth that the world provides, and the ontological truth of which Jesus speaks. Recall that Aristotle had told us that when we make, we want to make what is beautiful; when we do, we want to do what is good; and when we know, we want to know what is true. Thus, truth, from Aristotle's perspective, and the common perspective of Western Christianity has been largely epistemic or a matter of knowing what is true without much concern for what is beautiful or good. When Jesus, however, tells us that he is "the way, and the truth, and the life,"[16] he is not talking about an epistemic truth that is simply something to know and believe because it is true, but an ontological truth that is something to be because it is divinely beautiful and good, as well as true. The ontological truth of which Jesus speaks is the ultimate truth of who God created us to be. It is the unchanging, eternal truth of who God is calling us to be. By contrast, truth as something to merely know is constantly changing.

---

16. John 14:6.

In the late medieval world, nearly everyone believed that Aristotle had given us a comprehensive understanding concerning how the world worked. That understanding dominated Western thinking for several hundred years. At the beginning of the seventeenth century, however, the invention of the microscope revealed that there was much more to the world than Aristotle could have imagined. In time, Isaac Newton explained that much larger world with mathematical accuracy, and the poet Alexander Pope (1688-1744) wrote: "Nature and Nature's laws lay hid in night: God said, Let Newton be! and all was light." Finally, we had the *truth* about the world, but then Albert Einstein (1879-1955) explained that Newton was wrong, and time and space were not two different things but parts of the same thing; and the world became mysterious again. Today, Quantum Theory has discovered ever smaller entities that seem to more resemble elements of consciousness, rather than matter.

In light of our history, it seems irrational, or at least naïve, to believe that at some point we will get beyond apparent truth or truth as it appears to us from a certain perspective, and we will know truth independent of our perspective. Truth, as something to know, however, will always be an interpretation based upon the conceptual understanding through which we interpret the data of our experience. Of course, without an understanding of history, it is all too easy to believe "that the truth is the truth" and what we believe is true because we are not aware of any other way of conceptualizing the data in question. This is the basis for fundamentalism and what divides the world into warring cultural tribes, because people are unable to imagine the world differently from the understanding they inherited from their particular socio-cultural world. Throughout history, most people had little exposure to cultures and historical epochs that were not their own. Without such exposure, there is little to challenge one's inherited understanding of the world. Only recently has liberal education and travel exposed large numbers of people to ideas and experiences that stand as anomalies to the understanding they initially inherited. Without such experiences it is easy to imagine that our interpretation of data is not an interpretation at all, but the way things actually are. This is the way most human beings throughout history have understood truth and we see this concept of truth revealed in the Bible. Biblical truths begin as the apparent truths of an ancient tribal people who eventually have that understanding changed by prophets who have deeper, right-brain experiences with God that challenge the inherited apparent truths that are generally maintained and enforced by the priestly caste.

The ancient Jews were a tribal people; and their perspective of everything, including God, was tribal. Their God was not the same as the God of the people on the other side of the river, and therefore they could kill the babies in Jericho, since those were not the babies of their God. Of course, when the great Jewish prophets arose, they condemned the people for doing what earlier people believed was what God had ordained.

The Bible, as God's revelation of his relationship with human beings, reveals a spiritual journey whereby human beings encounter the Divine and all too quickly imagine that they know God and what God wants. We are always premature in what we claim to know. I remember an author recounting a story about when she was four years old and told her mother, "I think I now know everything I need to know." Her mother responded, "No you don't," and the child responded, "I think I do." We never fully outgrow that sense that we now know all that we need to know, but truth, in terms of what we claim to know, is always an apparent truth, and there is always a better perspective. This is especially true when it comes to knowing God and ourselves.

Our recent history has brought us to understand that our human experience is a composite of both the data of our experience, and the unique way we have been taught to interpret that data. We may all begin with a very similar God-given ability to interpret the data of our experience in a way that distinguishes our experience from that of other animal species. That data, however, is also interpreted through historical, cultural, linguistic, and personal perspectives that filter our experience into our own unique understanding. Our early education is a matter of receiving filters appropriate to our time and place in human history in order to make our understanding common to our particular cultural tribe. As children, we believe that what we are learning is the way the world actually is. In time, however, we come to experience, through books and personal encounters, people with different historical and cultural perspectives. At such points, we either choose to see our interpretation as better than the ones we are encountering, or we adapt our understanding to accommodate those parts of other peoples' perspectives that we see as superior to our own. If the other person's cultural perspective is radically different from our own, we most often ignore what that other person has to say, because it makes no sense from the perspective of our understanding.

In our reading of the Bible, we love those portions that make sense from our perspective in the world, and we tend to ignore those parts of scripture that don't make sense. Not surprisingly, those portions of the Bible that we most frequently ignore are the things that Jesus actually said. Indeed, from our perspective in the world, the things that Jesus says make no sense. Do you really believe that it makes sense to: "Love your enemies and pray for those who persecute you"[17]? Who believes that it makes sense to "give to everyone who begs from you"[18]; or that it is a good idea to "sell all that you own and distribute the money to the poor"[19]; or that we should consider ourselves blessed "when people revile you and persecute you and utter all kinds of evil against you"[20]? Do you really think it is a good idea to "…not resist an evil doer. But if anyone strikes you on the right cheek, turn the other also"[21]? These things that Jesus says are absurd from our inherited per- spective in the world. Other portions of scripture may speak to who we are in the world, but Jesus is usually addressing who he is calling us to be in his kingdom, rather than who we are in the world. That requires a radical change of perspective.

Jesus' truth is not like the apparent truths of science, religion, or economics. Our scientific theories, religious doctrines, and eco- nomic beliefs are all susceptible to the vicissitudes of time and our ever changing perspectives. Jesus' words, however, represent the eternal truth of who God is calling us to be. The Gospels do not tell us what to believe but how to be. Jesus' words are the Rock of Ages toward which all of human history continues to ever so

17. Matthew 5:44.
18. Matthew 5:42.
19. Luke 18:22; Also Matthew 19:21.
20. Matthew 5:11.
21. Matthew 5:39.

slowly evolve. Jesus' truth is not something to merely know and believe. His truth is the truth of the human species. It is the truth of who God created us to be, and we move ever closer to that divine way to be by internalizing Jesus' words, and making them our own, in order to be changed into his likeness. For that to happen, we have to loosen our grip on our apparent, epistemic truths and allow God to draw us through prayer and Jesus' words into the fullness of life that is the gospel. That requires that we become comfortable with the liminal space of not knowing. Liminality refers to that transitional space between what was and what is next. Liminal space is where all transformation takes place and it is the place to which Jesus' words are always calling us. Liminal space is where the understanding through which we usually inter-pret the world no longer works, and we need that larger mind and that larger truth to which Jesus' words call us.

Jesus, like all of the Jewish prophets, lived in the liminal space between his inherited understanding, and the things he was hearing from his Father in prayer. Likewise, his followers are called to that same liminal space between the inherited under-standing they receive from the world and Jesus' words. Our inher-ited understanding is true in that it is part of the spiritual journey that constitutes the ontological truth of our being. Jesus perfectly models the truth of the spiritual journey, which takes place in the liminal space between two worlds and two truths. The one truth is the apparent, epistemic truth that we inherit from the world, and the other is the ultimate, ontological truth to which Jesus' words call us. They are both places on the spiritual journey and part of the ontological truth of our being, which is ultimately determined by how much of Jesus' words we make our own.

Jesus is the alpha and the omega: the reason it all came into being and the end toward which all of history ever so slowly moves. As such, the truth of Jesus' words is seldom compatible with the cultural understanding we inherit from the world. From our inherited perspective in the world, it is foolish to love our enemies and give to all who ask. If, however, we spend time in God's presence and come to identity with that presence rather than the world, something begins to happen, and we begin to see Jesus' words as the most beautiful words ever spoken.

The basis for Jesus' truth is different from the basis for the epistemic truths that we claim to know and believe. The epistemic truths concerning what we claim to know are inherited from the world and validated by the fact that we believe what everyone else from our cultural tribe believes. The epistemic truths of what we claim to know are common, but Jesus' words are personal. They address the truth of our being rather than the truth of what we claim to know and believe. Jesus' words are things to be rather than doctrines to believe. His words are instructions to his disciples in order that they might be as he is. As such, they require a different mind or a different level of consciousness than the one we have inherited from the world. Indeed, his words only make sense from that deeper level of consciousness that we experience in prayer. When we are alone with God, we can see how beautiful and good Jesus' words are, but from our perspective in the world, they make little sense. Thus, without a regular practice of spending time alone with God in prayer, ignoring Jesus' words will be inevitable.

Jesus' words are not intended to benefit us in the world. They are meant to create the nature of our eternal being. His words do not represent epistemic truths that we add to our left-brain's understanding of the world. Jesus' words are the existential truth of our ultimate being. They are not things to know but things to become because they represent the ultimate form of human beauty and goodness. From our perspective in the world, however, Jesus' words appear neither beautiful nor good. Indeed, they are meant to shape the nature of our eternal being, and not our being in the world.

Knowing some of the things that Jesus said as part of our religious understanding is very different than having those words take root at the core of our being in order to make us into his likeness. As such, his words are enormously different from the words the world has given us in order to make us into its likeness. His words, when taken seriously, change the form of our being, and not merely our beliefs, but they are not words that make sense to our left-brain's understanding of the world. Indeed, his words require the rich soil of our soul in order to take root. The ultimate purpose of prayer is to access that level of consciousness where Jesus' words make sense and become the basis for our being.

God is interested in our being and not in what we claim to know and believe. Furthermore, God is interested in our eternal being and not our being in the world. Knowing God is not something that happens in our left-brain like the rest of our knowing. Knowing God is the ineffable, existential experience of being without knowing. The practice of experiencing that ineffable experience of *being* itself is what prepares the soul to receive the words of Jesus. The question is how much of Jesus' word do we want to receive and make our own? How real do we want his words to be in our life? Everyone wants to be forgiven by Jesus, but Jesus tells us that God's desire is not that we would simply be forgiven, but that we would become forgiving. "If you do not forgive others, neither will your Father forgive your trespasses."[22] God is in the business of making us into his forgiving likeness and not merely handing out forgiveness in exchange for whatever religious beliefs are in vogue at a particular time and place in human history. Religious beliefs and doctrines come and go, but the words of Jesus are the Rock of Ages that Jesus tells us to build our lives upon.

> Everyone then who hears these words of mine and acts on them will be like a wise man who built his house on rock. The rain fell, the floods came, and the winds blew and beat on that house, but it did not fall, because it had been founded on rock. And everyone who hears these words of mine and does not act on them will be like a foolish man who built his house on sand. The rain fell, and the floods came, and the winds blew and beat against that house, and it fell—and great was its fall![23]

The shifting sands of doctrines and theologies come and go, but the words of Jesus remain forever. "Heaven and Earth will pass away, but my words will not pass away."[24] Jesus' words are living words and are intended to make us into the eternal creatures God is calling us to be. Jesus' words are nothing like the epistemic truths of religious doctrines and theologies, which purport to make us righteous through our beliefs. The righteousness

---

22. Matthew 6:15, also see Mark 11:26.
23. Matthew 7:24-27.
24. Matthew 24:35.

of which Jesus speaks is the result of his followers making his words their own in order to be made into his likeness. His words address our being and not our beliefs. They tell us of the best and most beautiful way to be. Of course, the problem with his words is that they tell us of a way to be that is radically different from the way the world has told us to be. In fact, if we pay attention to Jesus' words, and allow them to take root within us, they draw us to that deeper level of being *in* God rather than being in the world. Indeed, Jesus' words, when taken seriously, will destroy the faith we have in our own understanding because they address the truth of our being rather than the truth of what we claim to know and believe. Our religious doctrines and beliefs are what connect us to the world, while Jesus' words are meant to set us free from the world. Our religious doctrines and theologies are part of our left-brain's understanding of the world. Jesus' words cannot take root in the understanding the world has given us, because they are not things to know and believe because they are true, but things to become because they are divinely beautiful and good.

Who we are in the world can claim to know Jesus, but being known by Jesus because his words are growing within us requires a different mind, a different level of consciousness, or as Jesus says a new wineskin. The new wine of the gospel cannot be put in the mind we inherit from the world. It requires the new mind to which Jesus calls us, but as Jesus says, our response is most often, "the old is good enough"[25] Many Christians believe that their faith in their religious tradition is good enough. That was what the religious leaders of Jesus' day thought as well, but God

---

25. Luke 5:39.

is not interested in our religious beliefs. God's ultimate desire is that we would become the ultimate truth of who God made us to be, which Jesus models and his words proclaim.

Jesus' life, death, and resurrection are mysteries that can be experienced but are never reducible to something as base as theories constructed out of words. Our theories, whether scientific, religious, or economic, are all human constructs, and although they can be helpful concerning our life in the world, they do not address the truth of who we ultimately are called to be in God. The truth of our being is not determined by what we profess to believe, but who we are, which is determined by what we love. Do we love the world and the things that it tells us to love in order to be happy, or do we love the words of Jesus and the things he tells us to love in order to find the divine happiness to which Jesus calls us?

The ultimate purpose of the gospel is to establish an identity in God rather than an identity in the world. That is the end of the spiritual journey and what it means to be a disciple of Jesus. As such, the gospel is not something to believe but something to become. Beliefs tend to be static, which gives them the appearance of certainty, but the gospel of Jesus' words is dynamic and meant to bring us into an ever-deepening personal relationship with God. In truly personal relationships, our understanding of the other person, as well as our understanding of ourselves, is constantly changing, and if our understanding is not changing we are not in a personal relationship with that other person. Many marriages are not personal relationships because both parties have made up their minds about who the other person is, and they no longer have to experience that other person, which might reveal anomalies to what they claim to know about that other person.

Likewise, if our concept of God has not changed over the last few years, we do not have a personal relationship with God; we just have a left-brained belief system. Our over-identification with the left-brain's knowing is what causes us to miss out on the deeper experiences that come out of the openness of mind that not knowing involves.

What is nice about having a static belief system about God, rather than a personal relationship, is that if God doesn't change, we don't have to change either. When someone says, "My mind is made up", what they mean is their mind is closed to any experiences that might present anomalies to what they claim to know and believe. Of course, at early stages in life we want our children's minds to be made up in order for them to get the kind of security that comes from believing that they know certain things about the world and how it works. When my daughters were young and would come home from school and tell me about something they had learned that day, I often would mention that there was another view or perspective concerning what they had learned. Initially, their response was, "No, Daddy! The teacher said!" The liminality that opens us to anomalous experiences only comes with maturity, but we all get to choose how far we want to go with this maturity that is the spiritual journey.

Faith, as a matter of our minds being made up, is a very early place in the spiritual journey. In order to maintain that place we have to avoid Jesus' words, since his words are constantly calling us to repentance. The Greek word that the Gospels use, which is translated as repentance, is *metanoia*. The Greek prefix *meta* is after or beyond, and *noia* refers to mind or thought. Repentance is a matter of constantly changing our minds in order to accommodate the words of Jesus. We only acquire the words of Jesus for ourselves, as we take on the mind of Christ. The mind of Christ is the mind we are constantly coming into because we are serious about making Jesus' words our own.

Jesus did not come into the world to give us a belief system that opens us to God's forgiveness. God is not ultimately interested in forgiving us. God is ultimately interested in making us into his forgiving likeness because God knows that ultimate happiness can only be found in our becoming like God in terms of forgiveness and love. Being forgiven is not the end game. Being made into Jesus' forgiving likeness is the end game. Forgiving the sins of others is what sets us free. Believing that God is selective in his forgiveness is what allows us to be selective in our forgiveness of others. Jesus, from the Cross, prays for his torturers to be forgiven.[26] That should be enough to convince us that there is no place in God for unforgiveness and there should be no place in us for unforgiveness. We all want to be forgiven, but being forgiven only gets us half way. It gives us the belief that God wants to forgive us because of something we have done or believed, rather than because God wants to make us into his forgiving likeness.

Of course, we can only see as much of God as we are open to seeing. Our fixed and certain religious beliefs are what keep us from seeing more of God. In scripture these are often the religious zealots that kill the prophets because the prophets speak of a deeper relationship with God. Jesus' words are always personal and speak to either where we are at or where Jesus is calling us to be. When Jesus speaks to the religious leaders of his day, he is

---

26. Luke 23:34

speaking to where they are at; but when he speaks to his disciples he is speaking to where he is calling them to be. The words that he speaks to his disciples cannot be heard from the perspective of those religious types that equate the forgiveness of sins with righteousness. The words that Jesus speaks to his disciples reveal our sin at ever greater depths in order that we might remain open to God's forgiveness and mercy, which transforms us into his forgiving and merciful likeness. What stops the transformative flow of his forgiveness and mercy is our idea that God's forgiveness of our sins makes us righteous. Righteousness, as a belief, is very different from righteousness as a becoming by seeing our sin and need for repentance at ever deeper levels by paying attention to Jesus' words. Jesus tells a parable about this.

> When the unclean spirit has gone out of a person, it wanders through waterless regions looking for a resting place, but not finding any, it says, 'I will return to my house from which I came.' When it comes, it finds it swept and put in order. Then it goes and brings seven other spirits more evil than itself, and they enter and live there; and the last state of that person is worse than the first. [27]

Forgiveness removes the unclean spirit, but if we equate the forgiveness of sin with righteousness, we open ourselves to the evil spirits that love to dwell in the righteousness of religious people. If we believe that our beliefs have made us righteous, we are no longer open to repentance in response to Jesus' words and the constant flow of God's forgiveness and mercy. Becoming God's

---

27. Luke 11:24-26, also see Matthew 12:43-45.

forgiveness and mercy to the world is Jesus' idea of righteousness, but we only enter into that righteousness by seeing our sin and need for forgiveness and mercy at ever deeper levels.

Our religious beliefs are merely part of our left-brain's understanding of the world. Jesus' words are the words of eternal life. They are always calling us to something deeper than mere beliefs. Jesus' words are things to experience at a deeper level of consciousness than that level of consciousness that connects us to the world. This is the repentance, or the changing of our mind that lies at the heart of the gospel message. It is not merely remorse over sin but a change from one mind and identity to another. It is a matter of changing our minds from who the world says we are, to who Jesus says we are. Many who identify as Christians claim to have been born again and are now a new creation, but, for many, their identity is still in the world. They identify themselves the way the world identifies them, rather than by identifying with Jesus' words and the heavenly virtues those words produce when seriously ingested into our being. Identifying with Jesus' words requires that we dis-identify with all those things that attach us to the world and keep us from the fullness of life to which Jesus calls us.

Jesus' words are meant to constantly draw us to repentance or the changing of our mind from the mind the world has given us, to the mind that is open to Jesus' words. This is the mind we are capable of experiencing in prayer. It is not the knowing mind of the left-brain, but the apophatic, experiential mind that is able to recognize Jesus' words as anomalies to the understanding the world has given us. It is only our openness to the anomalous nature of Jesus' words that have the capacity to change us into his likeness.

Of course, we seldom begin there. We usually begin the spiritual journey with the epistemic beliefs about God that we inherit from our particular socio-cultural world. Those beliefs, however, are never compatible with Jesus words. That is because our initial beliefs about God are from the perspective of who God appears to be from the subject/object perspective that we have inherited from the world. From that perspective, God is the ultimate object that we have to learn to appease and manipulate through our worship, obedience, right beliefs, and behavior. Thus, our initial relationship with God is usually one of meritocracy where we imagine that good people are rewarded and bad people are punished. Jesus' words, however, are never about that kind of religious righteousness. Jesus tells us that "there will be more joy in heaven over one sinner who repents than over ninety-nine righteous persons who need no repentance."[28]

We almost all begin the spiritual journey with a desire to be right before God, and religions are quick to give us formulas for such righteousness. We imagine that God must be like us and is offended by our sin, just as we are offended by those who sin against us. So we are careful not to sin, and when we do, we have a formula whereby that sin can be forgiven and removed. Sin, however, is not something to be eliminated in order to make us righteous before God, but something to see at ever deeper levels in order for God's forgiveness and mercy to continue to flow through us in order to make us ever more forgiving and merciful. This is the thing that religious people are generally missing and Jesus tells us we need to go in search of and find.

---

28. Luke 15:7.

The spiritual journey is about seeing that we are missing something and we need to go in search of it. In the fifteenth chapter of Luke's Gospel, the entire chapter is about being lost, and how being lost is a good thing and not a bad thing. Of course, like all of Jesus' teachings there is not a single or ultimate meaning but the meaning changes depending upon where we are at in our transformation into his likeness. Our initial interpretation of Jesus' words is usually from our inherited cultural understanding. From our perspective in the world it is not a good thing to get lost, but from the perspective of our identity in God, it is the essential thing in order to be found by God at ever deeper levels. Getting lost is necessary in order to be found.

In this chapter of Luke's Gospel about a lost sheep, a lost coin, and a lost son, the sheep got lost, and was not saved by its goodness but the goodness of the shepherd. Likewise, a lost coin has no value and its value is only restored by being found. Finally, with the story of the lost son, we see that we do not come to that deeper level of becoming merciful and forgiving by being righteous and obedient, as was the older brother, but by receiving the Father's mercy and forgiveness. The story of the Prodigal Son is the story of one son doing it wrong and that turning out to be good, and the other son doing it right, and that turning out to be bad. The story ends with the good, older brother refusing to go to the party his father is giving for his prodigal brother. The older brother is sinless and wants to have his righteousness rewarded, but what Jesus reveals in this parable is that the righteousness to which God calls us is not one of being obedient and sinless, but one of becoming forgiving and merciful for having received much forgiveness and mercy. Henri Nouwen (1932-1996) claimed that if you get the story of the prodigal, you get the gospel; and if you don't get the story of the prodigal, you don't get the gospel.

Of course, like all great stories it appeals on multiple levels, and those levels are usually indicative of where we are at in the spiritual journey. How often have you read the story of the Prodigal and sympathized with the good, older brother who now has to share his father's diminished estate with his sinful brother? The goodness of the older brothers is being punished and the sin of the prodigal is being rewarded. That is not good from the perspective the world has given us. From our perspective as good religious people we want obedience to be rewarded and disobedience punished, or at least that is usually the perspective that we have early on in the spiritual journey. The end of the spiritual journey is to be filled with the father's forgiveness and mercy, rather than the righteousness of the older brother. This is why Jesus says, "Go and learn what this means, 'I desire mercy, not sacrifice.' For I have come to call not the righteous but sinners."[29] Only the sinner is open to the transformative power of God's mercy and forgiveness, and that is why Jesus' words are always telling us that our sin is deeper than we imagine. Jesus' words are constantly showing us that there is so much more to the fullness of life to which he calls us, but that fullness of life involves a very different way to be than the way the world has taught us to be. Our sin, or what keeps us from the fullness of life to which Jesus calls us, is that we love the world and its ways, rather than the ways to which Jesus' words call us. The Prodigal's older brother was good according to the ways of the world, and he wants to have his goodness rewarded

---

29. Matthew 9:13.

according to the ways of the world, but Jesus' words are always telling us of ways that are higher than the world's ways.

Jesus' words are always speaking against the world's notion of righteousness and pointing toward the heavenly righteousness of forgiveness, mercy, and love. The epistemic truths of our religious doctrines promise righteousness, but Jesus' words are always calling us to something deeper than righteousness. "The son of man came to seek out and to save the lost."[30] Make sure you never lose that sense of being lost in order to be found on the ever deeper levels to which Jesus' words call us.

The popular gospel preaches righteousness through the forgiveness of sins, but Jesus preaches a deeper repentance that leads to the kingdom virtues of the Gospels. The older brother of the prodigal son believes he is righteous because he is sinless, unlike his younger brother; but he doesn't see the kingdom virtues of forgiveness and mercy that he is missing. He is careful to avoid sin in order to be righteous according to the beliefs of his religious culture, but Jesus' words are always calling us to a deeper repentance in order that the divine virtues of forgiveness, mercy, and love might shape our eternal being.

---

30. Luke 19:10.

CHAPTER THREE

Knowing and Being

As we have said, Jesus' words are not things to know but things to experience in order to be transformed by them into his likeness. Knowing is a left-brain activity that reduces experience to words that can be mapped into theories and beliefs that are compatible with our inherited understanding of the world. If we trust the maps and theories that our left-brain provides, God can be reduced to a knowable object to be obeyed, revered, and worshipped. If, however, we are able to still our left-brain's rush to translate our experience into something knowable, *we can experience an unknowable oneness with God that exceeds our understanding, but not our experience.*

The right-brain, or whatever part of us is capable of experiencing phenomena without the kind of judgment and interpretation that the left-brain is so quick to provide, is the very thing that brings us into the raw experience of God. The raw experience of God is not something to be translated into knowing. Likewise, the words of Jesus are not things to know, but, as we have said, things to behold. Beholding is a way of experiencing beauty and goodness before it is processed through the conceptual understanding of the left-brain. Beholding is a state of being rather than a state of knowing. It is the state of being present to something in order to really take it in. We are seldom in such a state in the normal business of our lives. We generally operate almost unconsciously by processing the data of our experience through the understanding the world has provided. This is why we seldom hear or pay attention to the words of Jesus. If we have bought into the understanding we inherit from the world, the words of Jesus are nonsense. Loving your enemies and refusing to respond to violence with violence can get you killed. Obviously, Jesus is talking about some deeper level of being than our being in the world. That is why he tells us:

> Whoever comes to me and does not hate father and mother, wife and children, brothers and sisters, yes, even life itself cannot be my disciple.[31]

Everything that Jesus says to his disciples has to be understood in the context of the spiritual journey and the deeper life to which he is always calling us. Seventeen times throughout the Gospels Jesus says "follow me."[32] Following Jesus is all about the spiritual journey of becoming ever more like him by making his words our own. In order to realize that deeper life to which Jesus calls us, we have to be free from our life in the world. Jesus' words, at least when he is speaking to his disciples, are always addressing the deeper life of who we are in God rather than who we are in the world. Our fathers and mothers taught us how to be the way the

---

31. Luke 14:26.
32. Matthew 4:19; 8:22; 9:9; 16:24; 19:21; Mark 2:14; 8:34; 10:21; Luke 5:27; 9:23, 59; 18:22; John 1:43; 10:27; 12:26; 13:36; 21:19.

world had taught them to be. That is the place from which every generation begins the spiritual journey. How far we go on the spiritual journey is about how seriously we take Jesus' words, and how much we are willing to die to who we are in the world. What the world teaches every generation is that life is about *my* father and mother, *my* wife and children, *my* brothers and sisters, and *my* life. That is the illusion against which Jesus is always preaching. Nothing is our own, or of ultimate importance, except our *being*, and Jesus' words tell us how to *be* in God rather than how to be in the world. Jesus' ultimate teaching is that we have a true Father in heaven who has revealed to Jesus the true way we are to be.

Jesus does on occasion speak of God as "my Father,"[33] but his more common reference to God is as "our Father" or "your heavenly Father," which appears twenty-seven times throughout the Gospels.[34] This is the radical basis for the theology that Jesus introduces, and the blasphemy for which he was eventually killed. Religious people are generally comfortable with a distant God to be worshipped and obeyed, but a God that is our own Father, and everyone else's Father as well, is a little too personal and too demanding. God, as a distant sovereign, can require obedience, and punish disobedience, but God as our own Father desires what all good fathers desire; that is, that we would become like our Father in terms of virtue and character. Jesus shows us what that would look like, and we recoil. We want a God that allows us to

---

33. Matthew 26:39; John 8:49, 15:10.
34. Matthew 5:16, 45, 48; 6:1, 4, 6, 8–9, 14–15, 18, 26, 32; 7:11; 10:20, 29; 18:14, 35; Mark 11:25; Luke 6:36; 10:21; 11:13; 12:30, 32; 15:21; John 8:41; 20:17.

look like the world, rather than like Jesus, and today's more popular forms of Christianity allow for just that.

It is incredibly easy to avoid the words of Jesus, since from
the perspective of who we are in the world; we cannot even hear the
words of Jesus. That is because things that are incompatible with
our left-brain's inherited understanding of the world are immediately flagged and dismissed by the emissary that is our left-brain.
It is easy enough to avoid the words of Jesus simply by being
in the world and trusting the understanding the world has given
us. Jesus' words are always incompatible with that understanding,
since Jesus' words, at least when he is addressing his disciples, are
always addressing who we are in God rather than the person we
are in the world. In the world, we operate according to the understanding the world has given us. We actually have two operating
systems: one is about our individual survival and prosperity in the
world, and the others about our relationship to God and all other
human beings. From the subject/object perspective of the person
we are in the world, our enemy looks nothing like us, but from
the perspective of our unitive consciousness, which we are able
to experience in prayer, we are able to see our enemy as the same
child of God as ourselves. They are only seen as different from us
by the understanding the world has given us. Of course, if our only
understanding and perspective is the one the world has given us,
and we never go to that deep place of prayer where we experience
our oneness with God and his creation, religion is just a matter
of who we imagine God to be from our cultural perspective. Our
claim that our religious beliefs allow us to know God is what has
created over forty thousand Christian denominations world-wide.

Jesus, however, is always speaking to the deepest levels of our being rather than our knowing. It is popular to believe that what we know and believe puts us in a right relationship with God, but our knowing is the very thing that keeps us from the deeper experiences of God. Our claim to know God is what ends the spiritual journey.

The experience of God's presence in prayer is a being experience and not a knowing experience. The unitive consciousness that connects us to God and God's creation is an ineffable experience and not something to know. It is that level of being that allows us to love our neighbor, and even our enemy, as ourselves. Without that unitive consciousness that we experience in prayer, our God experiences are filtered through the understanding the world has given us. That understanding tells us that we are nothing like our enemies, while the raw experience of God's presence makes the idea of enemies seem silly and an invention of the false-self that we and the world have created. The false-self is the "they-self" or the self that they say we are. Of course, without the deep experience of our true self, or who we are in God at the core of our being, the false-self is the only self of which we are aware.

Jesus tells us that he is not interested in who the world says we are, but who God says we are. What keeps us from that fullness of life to which Jesus calls us is our over identification with the world and all the attachments that entails. This is why the raw experience of God's presence in prayer is so important. When we practice that presence enough, and come to identify with it rather than the world, our attachments to the world, which keep us from the fullness of life in God, begin to fall away; and we become free to be who God is calling us to be.

The unfiltered, raw experience of God's presence in prayer is the only thing that can give us the perspective from which to see the beauty and goodness of Jesus' words. This is why prayer, as that deeper level of consciousness that gets us beneath the understanding we have inherited from the world, is so important. From the perspective of who we are in God, the false-self, or who we are in the world, is seen as the fiction it is, and we begin to live out of that larger self of who we are in God. This was the level of consciousness that was common to the early, apostolic church.

> Now the whole group of those who believed were of one heart and soul, and no one claimed private ownership of any possessions, but everything they owned was held in common. With great power the apostles gave their testimony to the resurrection of the Lord Jesus, and great grace was upon them all. There was not a needy person among them, for as many as owned lands or houses sold them and brought the proceeds of what was sold. They laid it at the apostles' feet, and it was distributed to each as any had need.[35]

This is the kingdom-level of consciousness of which Jesus spoke, and it can be seen throughout the history of the world in varying degrees. Of course, along with this level of consciousness there has also always been that other level of consciousness that is more conducive to grounding our lives in the world. The more grounded we are in this world; the less likely we are to take the words of Jesus seriously. From the subject/object perspective the world has given us, it is impossible to love our neighbor as

---

35. Acts 4:32-35; Also see Acts 2:44-45.

ourselves. In the world, our subject/object perspective sees our neighbor as an object and different from ourselves. It is only in God's presence that we experience the unitive consciousness that connects us to the rest of creation and Being itself.

The love of which Jesus spoke is not possible from the subject/object perspective of the left-brain. It requires that level of consciousness that is capable of experiencing God's ineffable presence. If we never go to that place of experiencing God's presence and being apart from the world, we will identify with religions that tells us that all God cares about is that we have the right beliefs in order to have our sins forgiven. Jesus, however, did not preach the forgiveness of sins. He preaches the divine virtues of forgiveness, mercy, and love, which are things to become rather than things to believe. We want our relationship with God to be based upon our beliefs and behavior, but that is not the nature of a relationship with a Father/God. A Father/God loves all of his children, but desires that they would become like him in virtue and character in order to achieve the fullness of life. Those that come close to achieving the likeness of our Father are not loved anymore by God, nor are those that are far from God loved any less. God's love does not discriminate, and his desire is that our love would not discriminate either. Being God's love to the world is its own reward. That, however, is impossible to see from our perspective in the world. From the subject/object perspective of the false-self, or who we are in the world, we want to be the object of God's love because of something good or beautiful within us. God, however, loves us because he is "our Father" and he wants us to love others because they are our sisters and brothers.

In the world, we want to be the object of love, and we imagine that God must be like us and desires our love and worship as well. Of course, that is where we usually begin the spiritual journey, but if we pay attention to Jesus' words, we see that he is not telling us how to be the objects of God's love, but rather how to be the agents of God's love, mercy, and forgiveness. Being the agents of love, mercy, and forgiveness require a different perspective than the subject/object perspective the world has given us. Who we are in God is who God created us to be before the world got a hold of us, and before we began to develop the idea of ourselves as a separate entity different from the objects that surround us. Many people claim to know God, but knowing God from the subject/object perspective of the left-brain is different from the experience of being *in* God rather than being in the world. The experience of being in God requires a return to our original, unitive consciousness of being in another being, and having that other being care for all of our needs. This is the little child Jesus tells us we have to return to in order to enter the kingdom of heaven. "Truly I tell you, whoever does not receive the kingdom of God as a little child will never enter it."[36]

The false-self that we and the world create through the subject/object perspective can never enter the kingdom of heaven. That is because the false-self is not real but merely an identity that the world either projects upon us, or we attempt to project upon the world in order to control and manipulate our interaction with the world. Some people accept the identity the world imposes upon them, while others insist upon creating their own identity

---

36. Mark 10:15; Matthew 18:3.

and imposing it upon the world, but both are false-identities. Our true identity is in God and not in the world. This is the ultimate truth of Jesus' message and the truth of the gospel. Being *in* God is very different from claiming to know God from the subject/object perspective of the false-self. From the subject/object perspective the world has given us, God is yet another object to be dealt with, but from the unitive consciousness of being *in* God, God is *our Father* and the ultimate source of our being. When we start to see ourselves as being in God and part of Being itself, the subject/object distinction is lost and we experience what Jesus describes when he says, "On that day you will know that I am in my Father, and you in me, and I in you."[37] This experience of being in God and God being in you, just as Jesus was in God and God was in Jesus, is blasphemy from the subject/object perspective the world has given us, but it is the perspective to which Jesus is always calling us, and it is the only perspective from which to make sense of his words.

In the world, it is essential for us to be able to distinguish ourselves as different from the objects we encounter in the wild or crossing a busy urban street. Jesus, however, is not telling us how to be in the world, but how to enter his kingdom in order that we might experience the beauty and goodness of his words and be transformed by them. This is the deep state of prayer to which Jesus calls us. "But you, when you pray, go into your inner room, close your door and pray to your Father who is in secret, and your Father who sees *what is done* in secret will reward you."[38] This is

---

37. John 14:20.
38. Matthew 6:6. NAS

the deep state of prayer where we return to who we were in God before the world got a hold of us and began molding us after its ways.

In this deep state of prayer where we shut ourselves off from the world and experience our ineffable connection to God and his creation, rather than our connection to the world, we begin to see the beauty and goodness of Jesus' words. If we never go to this altered state of unitive consciousness, and we live our lives out of the subject/object perspective that the world has given us, and we will always ignore Jesus' words since they make no sense from the subject/object perspective that the world has given us. In order to see the beauty and goodness of Jesus' words, we have to spend time in that unitive consciousness from which we identify with being in God rather than being in the world. From the level of unitive consciousness, we are able to see how beautiful it is to love our neighbor, and even our enemy, as ourselves. Without identifying with this level of consciousness that we are able to experience in prayer, Jesus' words will always be ignored. This is why prayer as that altered state of unitive consciousness is so important, since it is the only thing that can prepare the soil of our soul to receive Jesus' words. Spiritual maturity is a matter of learning to live in the world from that prayerful state of consciousness where we are in the world, but no longer identify with who we are in the world.

Living out of the kind of unitive or non-dualistic consciousness that we experience in prayer requires a much greater level of faith than living out of a left-brain consciousness, which is constantly aware of our own particular needs, as distinct from everyone else's needs. As we have seen, the first century church seemed to have overcome that dualist thinking and they lived in communities where the distinction between oneself and others was lost, or at least greatly diminished. As Christianity spread, however, a less communal form of Christianity began to emerge. By the beginning of the third century, it had become obvious to some that the faith of following Jesus had become something quite different from its original intent. In order to rediscover the original, mystical and unitive consciousness of the apostolic church, the Desert Fathers and Mothers went into the Egyptian desert and created ascetic communities that would eventually evolve into the monastic traditions of the church.

By the fourth century, however, the Roman emperor Constantine (272-337AD) had converted to Christianity, and called for the council of Nicaea (325AD), which established the basic doctrines of the church. Doctrines are things to know and believe, whereas Jesus' teachings are always about ways to *be*, rather than merely things to believe. When a Roman Emperor endorses a set of beliefs and deems them to be what constitutes true Christianity, however, Christianity becomes something very different than what it had been for the earlier church which took Jesus' words seriously. This historical transformation of Christianity into a set of beliefs rather than a way of being became very popular, since it meant that Christianity could be practiced out of the same level of consciousness with which we interact with the world. As such, Christianity became a set of beliefs that could be known along with all of the other knowing the world has given us. This was very popular and along with other factors contributed to making Christianity the world's largest religion. The teachings of Jesus, however, and the kind of unitive consciousness that is able to make sense of those teachings, was replaced with a set of beliefs rather than a heavenly way to be. Christianity, as a set of beliefs rather than a prayerful level of consciousness that would allow Jesus' words to take root at the core of our being, became very popular, since it asks very little of us other than that we have the right beliefs and religious practices.

With Christianity as a set of doctrines to believe rather than a matter of Jesus' words taking root at the core of our being, heresy became the threat to this new notion of Christianity. The original intent of the gospel, however, was not completely lost. The monastic system that evolved out of the Desert Fathers and Mothers kept something of the non-dual consciousness of prayer alive, and provided the kind of life style that was more compatible with Jesus' teachings. The institutional church, however, largely became a belief system with the hierarchy of the church determining orthodoxy and who was in and who was out based upon one's beliefs.

Jesus' words, however, are always addressing our *being* in God rather than what we claim to know and believe. Knowing is something we can do without much effort, but transformation into a different kind of being is another matter. Knowing is something that happens on the surface of our being. The false-self is capable of knowing, but knowing is often what keeps us from going to those deeper levels of being from which we can see the beauty and goodness of Jesus' words.

Jesus spoke in parables, and Matthew's Gospel tells us that "without a parable he told them nothing."[39] Parables are stories that

---

39. Matthew 13:34.

contain deeper meanings, but in order to get to those deeper meanings, you have to recognize that you do not know the whole story, and you have to dig for the deeper meaning. With great literature there is always a deeper story, and with divine literature, there is an eternal depth to the story. Of course, we all get to choose the depth at which we wish to read the story. Thinking that the gospel is about Jesus being our savior is like thinking that Moby Dick is a story about a whale. We can read the Bible as a story about God sending his son into the world to suffer and die as payment for our sins, but, in order to stop at that level of knowing, you have to avoid the deeper story of the Gospels and Jesus' words.

Jesus says. "The reason I speak to them in parables is that 'seeing they do not perceive, and hearing they do not listen, nor do they understand.'"[40] We claim that we want to know, but we refuse to recognize that the first step to knowing the deeper truth of the Gospels is a matter of embracing the fact that we do not know. The humility of not knowing is the only way to those deeper levels of knowing and being that are able to hear Jesus' words and be transformed by them into his likeness.

I love the Dialogues of Plato where Socrates usually begins by claiming not to know the topic at hand, but as the conversation progresses, it becomes obvious that Socrates does know a great deal about the topic, but there is always more to know, which requires that apophatic level of consciousness that is so characteristic of the spiritual journey to which Jesus calls us. Although Socrates appears to know much more than most of his interlocutors, Socrates really does not know the way he would like to know.

---

40. Matthew 13:13.

By contrast, knowledge is always a construct that we create to end the inquiry and give us a false sense of security in the belief that "we know", but there is no end to the truth of the gospel. We will spend eternity exploring its depths.

Apophatic knowing is the "not knowing" that opens us to ever deeper levels of meaning. Kataphatic knowing is what reduces God to something that makes sense from our perspective in the world. Jesus' words never make sense from our perspective in the world, but only from the perspective of who we are in God. We do not know Jesus' words the way we know others thing. Jesus' words are living words meant to take root at the core of our being in order to make us into his likeness. It is not about knowing Jesus but about becoming Jesus' forgiveness and mercy to the world. Indeed, Jesus has very hard words to say about those who make a pretense to knowing him, without the deeper experience of his presence, which alone allow his words to take root within us.

> Not everyone who says to me, 'Lord, Lord,' will enter the kingdom of heaven, but only the one who does the will of my Father in heaven. On that day many will say to me, 'Lord, Lord, did we not prophesy in your name, and cast out demons in your name, and do many deeds of power in your name?' Then I will declare to them, 'I never knew you; go away from me, you evildoers.'[41]

We may boast of knowing God, but Jesus says it is not about our knowing God, but about Jesus knowing us. When Jesus says, "I never knew you", he is speaking of the kind of knowing of

---

41. Matthew 7:21-23.

which the Bible speaks when we are told that Adam knew Eve
and his seed produced new life within her.[42] Jesus' words are the
seeds of eternal life, as we will see in the chapter on the Parable
of the Sower, but those words cannot take root in the person we
are in the world. They require a different identity and a different
level of being.

This deeper level of being, which identifies with God rather
than the world, has never been popular among the larger number of those who consider themselves Christians. It had always
been kept alive, however, by a remnant: first by the Desert Fathers
and Mothers, than by the monastics, and then the great Christian
mystics of the late medieval period. Indeed, even the great ana-
lytic medieval thinkers like Thomas Aquinas (1225-1274) and
Bonaventure (1221-1274) had a serious mystical strain running
through their work. This deeper level of being in God rather than
being in the world seemed to have all but ended, however, with
the great Spanish mystics of the 16th century. Brother Lawrence
(1614-1691) and Madame Guyon (1648-1717) were the last flick-
ers of the Catholic mystic tradition, which in the modern period
was only kept alive by Quietists and romantic poets. Modern
Christianity became a kataphatic war of words to be decided by
whose words made the most sense from one's perspective in the
world. These wars of words between Protestants and Catholics
would eventually become actual wars with both sides killing other
human beings in the name of Jesus.

The religious wars of the early modern period took place in
what was dubbed the Age of Reason. Rene Descartes (1596-1650),

---

42. Genesis 4:1.

who is considered the father of the modern thinking that would dominate the seventeenth and eighteenth centuries, established his first principle of reason upon himself. His maxim, "I think therefore I am" established the basis for modern thinking by equating truth with certainty. Descartes claimed that the only thing of which we could be certain was ourselves as thinking subjects, since that was the only thing that could be known without doubt. Descartes claimed that this thinking subject that I am is all I can know with certainty, since even the doubting of myself as a thinking subject was evidence of its existence. Therefore, beginning with the truth of myself as a thinking subject, I have to carefully examine and evaluate the veracity of all the objects that are presented to my thinking self. To paraphrase Descartes, "Many times in sleep I have been deceived," so how do I know that the objects presented to my mind in my waking hours are not deceptions as well? Descartes would go on to develop a method that would attempt to eliminate all ideas that were suspect of being less than certain. Descartes, and the modern thinking that would follow him, would look to mathematics and reproducible empirical evidence for that certainty, and disregard any claim to truth that did not present itself through those means.

By equating truth with certainty, truth became exclusively something to know rather than something to be. The ancient search for the meaning of life, which was about the beautiful, the good, and the true, was reduced to merely knowing with certainty. As we have seen, when Jesus says that he is "the way, and the truth, and the life,"[43] he is speaking of the ontological truth of our being and

---

43. John 14:6.

not certainty. Of course, the problem with Jesus' words is that we read them through the mind the world has given us, and that mind is still largely the mind of Descartes, which we inherit as being part of the modern world. Thus, the truth that many Christians cling to is the modern truth that they are certain about Jesus being their savior, and that the truth of eternal life is had through our certainty concerning that belief, rather than falling in love with the beauty and goodness of Jesus' words.

This idea of truth as certainty would have an enormous effect upon modern religion. In order to compete with the growing popularity of modern science, many of the more recently formed versions of modern Christianity maintained that their basic beliefs were supported by reason as well, and if one's religious beliefs were not supported by rigorous reasoning, they were illegitimate beliefs. In 18th century Scotland, David Hume (1711-1776) was deemed an atheist, not because he didn't believe in God, but because he didn't believe that God could be rationally known as the Enlightenment defined knowing. By the 18th century, a claim to truth required either empirical or rational evidence, but that is a very narrow understanding of truth. There is a difference between knowing answers that correspond to facts or reason, and know-how. Knowing how to hit a golf ball is different from knowing the answer to a math problem. Knowing the gospel is more like hitting a golf ball than knowing math. To know how to hit a golf ball, you have to spend a lot of time trying to hit golf balls, and to know the gospel means that you have to spend a lot of time in God's presence and Jesus' words. Who has the time for that in our contemporary world?

Today, the popular forms of Christianity offer the attractive alternative of believing the right doctrine in order to get our sins forgiven. Prior to the modern period, salvation or knowing who was in and who was out with God was always left up to God's wisdom. Of course, there were theories about dying in a state of sin or a state of grace, but it would have been hard to find anyone who was certain of their being right with God simply through the doctrines they believed. That was a product of the modern, Cartesian mind that equated truth with knowing and knowing with certainty.

Furthermore, with the modern notion of truth as certainty, the truth of one's faith came to be seen as how certain one was about the doctrines one believed. The mystery of the Cross, which had long been something to behold and experience, was reduced to an epistemic belief that served as a formula for salvation. This was certainly attractive; since it allowed us to by-pass the unsettling words of Jesus that always call us to repentance and transformation. Making the gospel into an epistemic belief about the certainty of one's salvation, rather than the words of Jesus, meant that Christians could become comfortable with who they were in the world, and could avoid those crazy words of Jesus that are so contrary to the ways of the world. Christians becoming comfortable with who they were in the world was especially important to the rise of capitalism.

With the rise of capitalism in the 19th century, our left-brain thinking became evermore dominant. In 1776, Adam Smith (1723-1790) published, *An Inquiry into the Nature and Causes of the Wealth of Nations.* Smith had seen that the economic structure of the world had been changing. In the past, many economic decisions were made simply by tradition. A man didn't choose his occupation, but inherited it from his father. One's surname was often the inherited occupation of one's father, such as Cook,

Tailor, Baker, or Banker. Likewise, prices were often established by tradition as well. Throughout the modern period, however, enormous social changes were destroying many of those traditions and some thought there was need for a command economy where governments would have to step in and make economic decisions in the absence of tradition. Smith, however, claimed that there was no need for such rational intervention, since he had discovered rational principles at the base of this new emerging economic structure. Just as Isaac Newton had discovered rational principles at the base of the physical world, Smith claimed that he had discovered rational principles at the base of the economic structure of the world.

His claim was that an economy set free from both tradition and governmental commands would be governed by the interaction of natural laws that would self-regulate an economy. The two laws that Smith believed would self-regulate markets were the laws of supply and demand. Both laws were based upon the idea of self-interest in that when someone buys something, they want to buy it at the lowest possible price, and when someone sells something, they want to sell it at the highest possible price. The interaction between supply and demand is what creates markets, and Smith claimed that free markets would always move toward equilibrium or a balance between supply and demand. A shop owner with a number of items to sell will always want to sell those items at the highest possible price, while the people buying those items always want to buy them at the cheapest possible price. If the shop owner sets the price too high, people will seek those items elsewhere, but if he sets the price too low, he will miss out on additional profit. Thus, the self-interest of both buyers and sellers will adjust prices in the direction of an equilibrium between the supply and demand of any given product or service. If the demand for a particular item is greater than the available supply, the price of that product will increase, but if the demand for a particular item is less than the available supply, the price will decrease. Thus, free markets, although seldom at equilibrium, will always move in that direction because of self-interest.

> It is not from the benevolence of the butcher, the brewer, or the baker, that we expect our dinner, but from their regard to their own interest. We address ourselves *not* to their humanity but to their self-love, and never talk to them of our own necessities, but of their advantages.[44]

This idea of self-interest also led to the development of capital or wealth as surplus. Those who were good at selling at the highest price and buying at the lowest price began to acquire wealth or capital. Of course, this idea of capital or surplus had been around for a long time but it had always been determined by birth more than markets. In the past, wealth was acquired mostly by nobles and through war or pillaging. Now it would be acquired by calculating one's self-interest better than others calculated their self-interest.

Initially, this seemed to be contrary to the Christian idea of loving your neighbor as yourself, but this new capitalism got a spiritual boost from the Protestant Work Ethics of John Calvin (1509-1564) and John Knox (1514-1572). They emphasized the importance of being industrious rather than idle, which opened

---

44. Smith, Adam. *An Inquiry into the Nature and Causes of the Wealth of Nations*. Modern Library Edition. New York: Random House. 1937. P. 14.

people to temptation, and they also warned against loving the world's goods and pleasures. Thus, if an individual was industrious but did not spend the fruits of that industry on worldly pleasures, capital or surplus would be the result. Knox even added the virtue of thrift which went right along with increasing one's surplus or wealth. Thus, from the perspective of the Protestant Work Ethic, capital or wealth was no longer a mere sign of being rich, but of being Godly as well.

If wealth could be seen as a result of godliness, perhaps wealth was part of God's blessings. Medieval Christianity had seen poverty as a virtue and many of the religious order made poverty a condition for piety. Likewise, the medieval church made usury, or lending money in order to make money, a sin, based upon Jesus' teaching that we are to lend without expecting anything in return.

> If you lend to those from whom you hope to receive, what credit is that to you? Even sinners lend to sinners to receive as much again. But love your enemies, do good, and lend, expecting nothing in return.[45]

With this new Protestant Work Ethic, however, God blesses the faithful with wealth, and poverty is no longer seen as virtuous but as the result of sin; namely, not being industrious and spending money frivolously upon worldly pleasures. I recall hearing a famous Evangelical preacher say, "The worst message the poor of this country ever got was that poverty was not their fault." He then went on to say, "Poverty is the fault of the poor." Consequently,

---

45. Luke 6:35.

religion should encourage the poor to be industrious and frugal rather than to indulge the sin of the poor with charity.

From a certain perspective, this is certainly true, but it is only one of the perspectives to which human beings have access. Our bicameral nature gives us access to both the subject/object perspective which see the objects we encounter as different from ourselves, but we also have access to a unitive level of consciousness that is able to see our neighbor, and even our enemy, as ourselves. Jesus' teachings are always addressing this unitive level of consciousness. This is the level of consciousness that gives us access to the moral and spiritual side of our being.

The truth of our being has little to do with the doctrines that we profess to believe. Our being is much more determined by the perspective and level of consciousness out of which we choose to live. One hundred and twenty-nine years after Adam Smith had published *The Wealth of Nations*, Max Weber (1864-1920) published *The Protestant Ethic and the Spirit of Capitalism*, in which Weber claimed that when capitalism becomes detached from that level of consciousness that connects us to God and other human beings it reduces our being to winning at the cost of others.

> In the field of its highest development, in the United States, the pursuit of wealth, stripped of its religious and ethical meaning, tends to become associated with purely mundane passions, which often actually give it the character of sport.[46]

---

46. Max Weber. *The Protestant Ethic and the Spirit of Capitalism*. New York: Charles Scribner's Sons. 1958. P. 182.

Sport is all about winning at the cost of others losing, which is a big part of our being in the world and the survival instincts of our animal nature, but unless it is balanced with our unitive consciousness that connects us with God and other human, we are no more than animals devouring one another. A Christianity that is built upon the understanding the world has given us is the basis for the prosperity gospel, but that gospel has to avoid the words of Jesus, which constantly tell us how different earthly treasure is from the kind of treasure to which Jesus calls us.

> Do not store up for yourselves treasures on earth, where moth and rust consume and where thieves break in and steal; but store up for yourselves treasures in heaven, where neither moth nor rust consumes and where thieves do not break in and steal. For where your treasure is, there your heart will be also.[47]

Of course, many Christians will argue that they are storing up treasure in heaven, but that God is blessing them with wealth here on earth as well. That, however, is hard to defend in light of Jesus' statement in Luke's Gospel: "Woe to you who are rich, for you have received your consolation."[48] Furthermore, this is not an isolated passage but one that seems to represent Jesus' very consistent position on wealth and poverty. In the parable of the Sower, which appears in all three of the Synoptic Gospels, Jesus tells us, "As for what was sown among thorns, this is the one who hears the word, but the cares of the world and the lure of wealth choke

---

47. Matthew 6:19-21.
48. Luke 6:24.

the word, and it yields nothing."[49] Additionally, in Luke's Gospel, Jesus presents us with a parable about a man who sought wealth rather than God.

> The land of a rich man produced abundantly. And he thought to himself, 'What should I do, for I have no place to store my crops?' Then he said, 'I will do this: I will pull down my barns and build larger ones, and there I will store all my grain and my goods. And I will say to my soul, Soul, you have ample goods laid up for many years; relax, eat, drink, be merry.' But God said to him, 'You fool! This very night your life is being demanded of you. And the things you have prepared, whose will they be?' So it is with those who store up treasures for themselves but are not rich toward God.[50]

Of course, there is nothing objectively evil about wealth. Jesus' concern and warnings about it seem to center on the effect it has upon human beings. That is because money, in addition to being a means of exchange, and a store of value (capital), is also a measure of value. In today's world, we measure the value of nearly everything in dollars, including the value of human beings. In most people's thinking, our value and identity in the world increases with our wealth. Wealth along with power and fame are the ultimate values of today's world, and they are the things we pursue in order to increase our identity in the world. Jesus, however, is always preaching against the deceptive identities such things produce. Jesus is always calling us to our true identity in God rather than who we are in the world. The rich, powerful, and

---

49. Matthew 13:22; Mark 4:19; Luke 8:14.
50. Luke 12:16-21.

famous may profess to love Jesus, but it is difficult for them to achieve the identity to which Jesus calls us, since Jesus tells us that it is impossible to have an identity both in the world and in God.

> No one can serve two masters; for a slave will either hate the one and love the other, or be devoted to the one and despise the other. You cannot serve God and wealth.[51]

In another place he says, "If you wish to be perfect, go, sell your possessions, and give your money to the poor."[52] Of course, it is not the physical act of giving away your possessions that somehow puts you in a better place with God, but the spiritual detachment from possessions and the illusions of happiness they provide. It is not about a physical act of giving away all of our possessions, but about our spiritual detachment from such things.

Jesus is always calling us to an identity in God rather than an identity in the world. An identity in God requires a spirit of poverty that rejects the illusions of happiness that the world sets before us. The world's notions of happiness center upon adding substance to our identity in the world by increasing things like wealth, power, and prestige. These are the illusions that create the false-self, which is who we want other people to believe we are. Of course, that false-self is merely a projection of what we want other people to believe about ourselves. Our true self is only apparent to God and ourselves when we are in God's presence. If we avoid that presence, we can deceive ourselves into believing

---

51. Matthew 6:24; also see Luke 16:13.
52. Matthew 19:21.

that the false-self we project to the world is actually who we are. It is for this reason that Jesus says the poor are blessed. "Blessed are you who are poor, for yours is the kingdom of God."[53] He tells us, "The Spirit of the Lord is upon me, because he has anointed me to bring good news to the poor."[54] The message he has for the rich is harsh: "It is easier for a camel to go through the eye of a needle than for someone who is rich to enter the kingdom of God."[55] The only time that Jesus appears to have anything good to say about monetary wealth is in the parable of the talents in Matthew's Gospel.[56] That parable, however, is almost identical to the parable of the ten minas in Luke's Gospel.

> As they were listening to this, he went on to tell a parable, because he was near Jerusalem, and because they supposed that the kingdom of God was to appear immediately. So he said, "A nobleman went to a distant country to get royal power for himself and then return. He summoned ten of his slaves, and gave them ten pounds, and said to them, 'Do business with these until I come back.' But the citizens of his country hated him and sent a delegation after him, saying, 'We do not want this man to rule over us.' When he returned, having received royal power, he ordered these slaves, to whom he had given the money, to be summoned so that he might find out what they had gained by trading. The first came forward and said, 'Lord, your pound has made ten more pounds.' He said to him, 'Well done, good slave! Because you have

---

53. Luke 6:20.
54. Luke 4:18.
55. Matthew 19:24; also see Mark 10:23-25; Luke 18:24.
56. Matthew 25:14-30.

been trustworthy in a very small thing, take charge of ten cities.' Then the second came, saying, 'Lord, your pound has made five pounds.' He said to him, 'And you, rule over five cities.' Then the other came, saying, 'Lord, here is your pound. I wrapped it up in a piece of cloth, for I was afraid of you, because you are a harsh man; you take what you did not deposit, and reap what you did not sow.' He said to him, 'I will judge you by your own words, you wicked slave! You knew, did you, that I was a harsh man, taking what I did not deposit and reaping what I did not sow? Why then did you not put my money into the bank? Then when I returned, I could have collected it with interest.' He said to the bystanders, 'Take the pound from him and give it to the one who has ten pounds.' (And they said to him, 'Lord, he has ten pounds!') 'I tell you, to all those who have, more will be given; but from those who have nothing, even what they have will be taken away. But as for these enemies of mine who did not want me to be king over them—bring them here and slaughter them in my presence.'"[57]

In this parable it seems quite obvious that Jesus is speaking about Herod, who had gone off to Rome to be made king of the Jews, and that a delegation of citizen was sent to Rome asking that Herod not be made king. The end of the story is that Herod kills that delegation that did not want him to rule. Since this parable is so much like the parable of the talents in Matthew's Gospel, I assume both are speaking about Herod and not God. God does not reap where he does not sow. The two parables are almost identical except for using two different units of money: a mina was about

---

57. Luke 19:11-27.

three months of wages for a laborer, and a talent was more than fifteen years wages for a laborer.

Of course, there are examples of rich, powerful, and famous people whose identities were in God rather than in the world; just as there are numerous examples of ungodly poor people. The point, however, is that our wealth, power, and prestige adds greatly to the illusion of the false-self, which keep us from discovering who we are in God at the core of our being. We are distracted from our true identity in God by the illusions of the world's promise of happiness, which we are told can be found in wealth, power, prestige, physical beauty, or talent. Jesus tells us, "Be on your guard against all kinds of greed; for one's life does not consist in the abundance of possessions."[58] Indeed, such possessions are the things that possess us and keep us attached to the world and the illusions of the false-self or who we want other people to believe we are, rather than discovering who we really are in God at the core of our being. In order to escape the illusions of the false-self that we and the world have created, we need to practice an awareness of God's indwelling presence at the core of our being. Without such a practice, the world continues to own our soul, and the words of Jesus make no sense.

Of course, there is nothing wrong with the epistemic knowing that our socio-cultural world provides as long as it remains the emissary to the greater, ontological truth of our being, which Jesus' words are always addressing. The epistemic truths of the left-brain are the truths we share with others; Jesus' words are always personal and establish the ontological truth of our being

---

58. Luke 12:15.

in God rather than our being in the world. We are bicameral by nature and not merely in terms of our brain. We have both a life in the world and a life in God. We have a subject/object perspective through which to understand our life in the world, and a unitive perspective through which to understand our life in God. The extent to which we identify with one over the other is what creates the nature of our eternal being. Our eternal being is not formed by what we believe, but by how much we identify with who we are in the world, or how much we identify with who we are in God.

The truth of the gospel is not a religious doctrine to believe because it is true, but the transformative experience of the beauty and goodness of Jesus' words, and the desire to make those words our own and the basis for our being. The ultimate truth of our being is not established by the epistemic truths that we claim to know and believe, but by how much or how little of Jesus' words have taken root within us. In order for his words to become our own, we have to see how beautiful and good they are, but that cannot be seen from the perspective of the false-self or who we are in the world. Getting to that perspective from which we can see the beauty and goodness of Jesus' words is what prayer is all about.

CHAPTER FOUR

Prayer

Prayer is about getting to that level of not knowing from which we can hear the words of Jesus. All of our knowing is about how to be in the world. All of Jesus' words are about how to be in God rather than how to be in the world. As such, his words are incompatible with the left-brain's understanding that we have inherited from our socio-cultural world. That world, and the understanding it has given us, is also what gives us our initial notion of God, and for many people that is their last notion of God as well. We all get to choose how much of God we want – how much of God we are comfortable with. Our inherited understanding of the world is never comfortable with Jesus' words, so most who consider themselves Christians simply ignore them, and opt for doctrinal beliefs that are compatible with the norms and values of our inherited socio-cultural world. Those doctrines, however, are merely epistemic beliefs that eventually pass away in time just like the abstracted beliefs and theories of science. Our theological beliefs are intended to change God's mind about us; Jesus' words are intended to change our minds about God and ourselves. Prayer, as Jesus and the mystics understood it, is what gets us to the place from which we can hear those words. Jesus tells us that his words are not his own but what he has heard from the Father.

> The one who rejects me and does not receive my word has
> a judge; on the last day the word I have spoken will serve as
> judge, for I have not spoken on my own, but the Father who
> sent me has given me a commandment about what to say and
> what to speak. And I know that his commandment is eternal
> life. What I speak, therefore, I speak just as the Father has
> told me.[59]

Or,

> Those who love me will keep my word, and my Father will
> love them, and we will come to them and make our home
> with them. Whoever does not love me does not keep my
> words; and the word that you hear is not mine, but is from the
> Father who sent me.[60]

Jesus' words have to be heard from the same place from
which Jesus heard them. They cannot be heard from the perspective of who we are in the world, but only from the perspective of
who we are in God, which is what prayer is all about. Prayer is
about getting away from the world in order to hear Jesus' words,
just as he heard them from the Father. In order to do that, Jesus
tells us that we have to go into our inner room and shut the door
in order to be alone with God.[61] As we have seen, it is not a literal
inner room and a literal shutting of the door, but that deeper level
of consciousness which shuts out the world in order to experience God's presence and Jesus' words. This deeper level of

---

59. John 12:48-50.
60. John 14-23-24.
61. Matthew 6:6.

consciousness is not easily achieved, but requires a daily practice of prayer whereby we get far enough away from the world that we can hear the words of Jesus.

Only the silence of God's ineffable presence gets us far enough away from the world that we can hear and see the beauty and goodness of Jesus' words. When we are not in God's presence, we are in the world and our mind is the mind that the world has created. When we are able to get back to that deeper level of consciousness that we were in God before the world got a hold of us, we can see the beauty and goodness of Jesus' words. Someone might interject, "You mean when you *imagine* you are in God's presence, Jesus' words are the most beautiful words ever spoken." OK, when I imagine I am in God's presence, and no longer identifying with who I am in the world, Jesus' words are the most beautiful words ever spoken. What is faith but imagining things more beautiful and good than what the world has presented to us? Prayer is about imagining who we are in God in order to be able to hear the words of Jesus. Prayer is that level of consciousness that turns off our knowing and opens our imagination to see the beauty and goodness of Jesus' words. Prayer is not something we add to all of the other things we do in the world. Prayer requires that different level of consciousness that is able to see that it is good for our soul to love our enemies and refuse to respond to violence with violence. Such things are not usually conducive to our survival and not part of our knowing how to be in the world, but Jesus is not interested in telling us how to be in the world, but how to bring his kingdom to earth, by living a kingdom existence in the world.

In order to get to that deeper level of consciousness, which allows us see the beauty and goodness of Jesus' words, we have to stop the constant flow of thoughts, ideas, and feelings that connect us to the world and keep us from an awareness of God's presence. Prayer is about silencing all the data that constantly occupies our attention and keeps us from experiencing the presence of God. When we pray from our perspective in the world, we are usually petitioning God concerning our life in the world. At its deepest level, however, prayer has little to do with our life in the world, but is about our life in God coming forth as we begin to see the lie of the false-self that we and the world have created. This is prayer as Jesus and the mystics understood it. It is that altered state of consciousness where the self no longer draws its life from the world but from the ineffable experience of God's presence. It is what Jesus is talking about when he responds to the Pharisees in Luke's Gospel.

> Now when He was asked by the Pharisees when the kingdom
> of God would come, He answered them and said, "The king-
> dom of God does not come with observation; nor will they
> say, 'See here!' or 'See there!' For indeed, the kingdom of
> God is within you."[62]

We all came into the world with an ineffable, unitive aware-ness of our connection to God and another human being. That is our deepest level of consciousness that we are trying to get back to in prayer. It is a very different level of consciousness and perspec-tive than we have inherited from the world. The world constantly demands that we pay attention to the objects that surround us. Prayer is a matter of refusing to allow those objects to occupy our

---

62. Luke 17:20-21. NKJV

attention. One way to do that is to focus upon our idea of God. Of course, early on in the spiritual journey our idea of God is the world's idea of God. From that perspective, God is yet another object that the world teaches us how to manipulate in order to get what we want. From our deeper level of unitive consciousness and the ineffable experience of God's presence, however, all of the theological maps and religious doctrines that seem so important to who we are in the world, lose their hold upon us, and we are able to see the beauty and goodness of Jesus' words. This is the perspective that allows Meister Eckhart to say, "I pray God to rid me of God", and I might add: so I might hear the words of Jesus. The god of my religious doctrines is different from the God I experience at the core of my being, which explains the words of Jesus to me. God may be beyond our understanding, but how to be "in God" is what Jesus explains and what the Holy Spirit translates into our being rather than our understanding.

> I have said these things to you while I am still with you. But the Advocate, the Holy Spirit, whom the Father will send in my name, will teach you everything, and remind you of all that I have said to you.[63]

The role of the Holy Spirit is to teach us everything by reminding us of all that Jesus has said. In order to be open to the Holy Spirit and Jesus' words, we have to be detachment from the world and many of the religious beliefs the world has given us. The god of religion tells us that God loves people who believe and behave as we do. That was the nature of religion in Jesus' day and

---

63. John 14:26.

that has not changed. Religious beliefs are about changing God in order to get what we want. What do I have to believe to get God to love me? Jesus' words are about getting us to love God and other human beings. If God is "our Father" as Jesus says, there is nothing we can do to get God to love us anymore than he already does. That is the nature of Fatherly love, which is the kind of love that God wants to impart to us that we might love as he loves without restriction.

Today's popular form of Christianity tells its followers that God will bless their beliefs and religious practices with material prosperity; Jesus tells us that this is the great lie of the god of this world. The god of this world is the god of the false-self who promises wealth, power, and prestige if we would worship the things of this world rather than the things of God. Who we are in God's presence has nothing to do with who we are in the world. Unlike our identity in the world, which increases with wealth, power, and prestige, our identity in God is founded upon our freedom from such illusions and the identity of the false-self that such illusions create. Prayer is the place we go in order to escape such illusions and discover who we are in God at the core of our being. This is the kind of deep prayer that is capable of preparing the soil of our soul to receive the words of Jesus. If we visit this place of prayer enough, and begin to identity with who we are in God rather than the world, Jesus' words begin to make sense.

The words of Jesus are never appropriate to who we are in the world. They are kingdom words and are always at odds with the world. In order to hear them, we have to get away from the world and all that the world has taught us, including many of the religious beliefs in which we put our trust. This is why

Jesus had trouble with the religious people of his day. Religion generally gives us prescriptions for righteousness within the confines of our particular socio-cultural traditions, but the words of Jesus are always calling us to something deeper. Popular religions are always about telling us how to be righteous through our tribal beliefs and righteous behavior. This is the religious spirit against which Jesus was always preaching. Jesus is not interested in giving us a prescription for that kind of righteousness. He wants us to rest in God in order to hear his words, which can only be heard when we are away from the world and resting in God. Jesus has a great teaching on this, although most do not recognize it as an example of prayer. It is the story of Mary and Martha.

> Now as they went on their way, he entered a certain village, where a woman named Martha welcomed him into her home. She had a sister named Mary, who sat at the Lord's feet and listened to what he was saying. But Martha was distracted by her many tasks; so she came to him and asked, "Lord, do you not care that my sister has left me to do all the work by myself? Tell her then to help me." But the Lord answered her, "Martha, Martha, you are worried and distracted by many things; there is need of only one thing. Mary has chosen the better part, which will not be taken away from her."[64]

The better part is Mary's resting in God, and not taking the world seriously. When we are not silent and still before God, the world has a hold of us and we think and behave as the world has taught us to think and behave. Martha is in the world, but Mary has found that better place of resting at Jesus' feet and listening to

---

64. Luke 10:38-42.

his words. That is the ultimate place of prayer. The ultimate truth of our being is not who the world tells us we are, but who Jesus tells us we are. The person we are in the world, however, cannot hear his words. His words are directed at his disciples and can only be heard by his disciples. Being a disciple of Jesus is very different than believing that Jesus paid for your sins, although that is as far as most people want to go with Jesus. Only disciples want to really hear Jesus' words because they know that being like him will put them at enmity with the world.

Being a disciple of Jesus does not happen through a belief. It only happens through a transformation into a different kind of being – the kind of being that is able to give root to Jesus' words. Furthermore, becoming this new kind of being is not something that we do but something that God does as we give ourselves into God's hands through prayer. Spending time in the silence of God's presence is what prepares the soil of our soul to receive Jesus' words. As we have said, from our place in the world, Jesus' words make no sense; that is why we need a practice of getting away from the world in order to prepare a place to receive his words. This is the ultimate purpose of prayer. It is a daily practice of entering into the silence of God's presence so Jesus' words might begin to take root within us. If we develop a daily practice of spending time in the silence of God's presence, something strange begins to happen behind our backs. Over time, we begin to notice that the world no longer has the hold on us it once had. By spending time in God's presence and away from the constant distractions that our attachment to the world produces, we begin to see the programs for happiness that the world has set before us as the illusions they are.

As we have said, we access God's presence through that part

of our bicameral nature that gives us access to our imagination rather than our knowledge. Our knowledge gives us access to the world, but our imagination gives us access to what is beyond this world. Of course, our imagination can lead us into all sorts of things that are not Godly; that is why the only thing we are trying to imagine in prayer is the silence and stillness of God's presence. Our imagination sets us free from the world and can be frightening, but in prayer the only thing we are imagining is the silence and stillness of God's presence, which alone allows us to hear the words of Jesus. The ultimate purpose of prayer is to get far enough away from the world in order to hear Jesus' words. Our imagining the silence and stillness of God is what silences the world in order that we might experience the beauty and goodness of Jesus' words.

Of course, when we begin a practice of prayer in order to experience the silence of God's presence, which opens us to the words of Jesus, we are only able to achieve the silence for seconds at a time before another distraction enters our consciousness. Thomas Keating has a great way of explaining how to get to this deeper, unitive consciousness that we access through the silence and stillness of prayer. He tells us to imagine that our consciousness is a river and the individual thoughts that appear in our consciousness are boats on that river. Instead of focusing upon the passing boats, just let them pass without fixing our attention upon them, until the boats have all passed and only the river or pure consciousness remains. When we begin this practice of prayer, the river is full of boats and our attention goes from one boat or thought to another. We could avoid this by simply filling our time of prayer with words to keep our attention directed, but Jesus tells us not to do this.

> When you are praying, do not heap up empty phrases like the
> Gentiles do; for they think that they will be heard because
> of their many words. Do not be like them, for your Father
> knows what you need before you ask him.[65]

Praying with words is how the world has taught us to pray in order to get our worldly needs meet, but the silence of God's presence is what opens us to hearing Jesus' words, just as it opened Jesus to hearing his Father's words. "Whoever does not love me does not keep my words; and the word that you hear is not mine, but is from the Father who sent me."[66] Prayer is about hearing, and silence is the way we enter into that space from which we can hear the words of Jesus. The silence of God's presence, which we experience in prayer, is nothing like our experience in the world. Neither is it like thinking. It is more like *being* in its purest form. It is being aware without an object to focus our awareness upon, since God is more than we can think or imagine. The silence of prayer is what brings us into that clear mind that gives us access to the beauty and goodness of Jesus' words. What we experience in the silence of prayer is being in its purest form, untainted by the distractions that the world constantly provides in order to distract us from an awareness of God's presence, and our being *in* that presence. Being is not an object that demands our attention the way the things of the world constantly demand our attention. Being exists on a deeper level than knowing. When our lives are directed by the knowing of our left-brain, we never love our enemies, give to all who ask, or refuse to respond to violence with

---

65. Matthew 6:7-8.
66. John 14:24.

violence. When, however, we experience that deeper level of consciousness that gives us access to an awareness of the Divine presence at the core of our being, we see how beautiful it is to be the way Jesus calls us to be. This was the level of consciousness out of which Jesus experienced his oneness with the Father and he invites us into that same oneness in order that we might hear his words just as he heard them from the Father.

> For I have not spoken on my own, but the Father who sent me has himself given me a commandment about what to say and what to speak. And I know that his commandment is eternal life. What I speak, therefore, I speak just as the Father has told me.[67]

Jesus invites us into that same level of consciousness and tells us that God is not simply his Father, but "our Father" as well. At this we recoil. We might be willing to accept that Jesus and the Father are one, but we dare not enter into that same oneness ourselves. We claim that such intimacy would be prideful, and we choose to stay at a respectful distance from God as his humble servants. That seems right and holy, but it is just a disguise for our deeper sin of wanting to retain our lives in the world, rather than forsaking our lives in the world in order to experience the reign of God, just as Jesus did. Our deepest sin is that we do not want to get lost in God and his purposes for our lives. We just want God to help us fulfill our purposes; that is, the purposes and desires of the false-self that we and the world have created. In order to discover God's purposes for our lives, we have to get to that deeper level

---

67. John 12:49-50.

of being in God, but in order to get to that deeper level of being *in* God, the false-self or who we and the world have created has to die. "For those who want to save their life will lose it, and those who lose their life for my sake, and for the sake of the gospel, will save it."[68]

> Very truly, I tell you, unless a grain of wheat falls into the earth and dies, it remains just a single grain; but if it dies, it bears much fruit. Those who love their life lose it, and those who hate their life in this world will keep it for eternal life. Whoever serves me must follow me, and where I am, there will my servant be also.[69]

The death that Jesus calls us to is not the physical death of the martyr, but the death of the false-self or who we are in the world. Our life in the world is the great illusion of the false-self. As we have said, the false-self is the "they-self" or who they say we are. It is the self that holds both our righteousness and our shame. It is the branding that we receive from the world, and if we do not have a practice of getting alone with God on a regular basis, and identifying with who we are in the presence of the Divine, the false-self is all we have.

The prayers of the false-self are about making requests of God to bless our life in the world. The false-self wants God, but God at a distance, in order that the false-self might remain sovereign in order to pursue the illusions of happiness that the world sets before us. We want God, but we want the life we have created

---

68. Mark 8:35; Matthew 16:25; Luke 9:24.
69. John 12:24-26.

for ourselves in the world as well. Our false-self is our own creation, and that is the basis for our love of it. By contrast, our true self is God's creation before the world got a hold of us and began shaping us into its likeness. This is why Jesus tells us that we must be born again in order to return to our initial state of being in God rather than being in the world.

Only time in God's presence, and the way that presence illumines the words of Jesus, can convince us that the life to which Jesus calls us is immeasurably more than all the world can offer. Prayer is the way we access that different mind, or that apophatic level of consciousness that allows us to make sense of the words of Jesus. Prayer is what gives us access to that unitive consciousness of who we were in God before the world got a hold of us, and it is that unitive level of consciousness that gives us access to Jesus' words.

Doctrines and theologies are beliefs and exist on the epistemic level of things to know, but prayer is about that different level of consciousness that is able to experience *being* rather than thinking or feeling. Prayer is that place we go to in order to be intoxicated with God, because the world no longer has a hold on us. If our prayer life is not intoxicating we are still praying out of our identity in the world, and not out of who we are in God. As we descend into that deeper level of consciousness that is prayer, we are raised above all those concerns we have about our being in the world.

> Therefore I tell you, do not worry about your life, what you will eat or what you will drink, or about your body, what you will wear. Is not life more than food, and the body more than

clothing? Look at the birds of the air; they neither sow nor reap nor gather into barns, and yet your heavenly Father feeds them. Are you not of more value than they? And can any of you by worrying add a single hour to your span of life? And why do you worry about clothing? Consider the lilies of the field, how they grow; they neither toil nor spin, yet I tell you, even Solomon in all his glory was not clothed like one of these. But if God so clothes the grass of the field, which is alive today and tomorrow is thrown into the oven, will he not much more clothe you—you of little faith? Therefore do not worry, saying, 'What will we eat?' or 'What will we drink?' or 'What will we wear?' For it is the Gentiles who strive for all these things; and indeed your heavenly Father knows that you need all these things. But strive first for the kingdom of God and his righteousness, and all these things will be given to you as well.

So do not worry about tomorrow, for tomorrow will bring worries of its own. Today's trouble is enough for today.[70]

Prayer is the way we get to this state of consciousness that Jesus describes. The practice of prayer is the practice of our *being* consciousness, rather than our *knowing* consciousness; our knowing is what connects us to the world; our being is what connects us to God. Knowing is what the left-brain does through the dualistic, subject/object perspective that perceives us as different from everything else. Prayer, at its deepest level, reveals another Being not as an object outside of us but dwelling at the deepest recesses of our being. Christians refer to it as the indwelling of the Holy Spirit; and prayer, at its deepest level, is the experience of that

---

70. Matthew 6:25-34.

indwelling Divine presence. Again, this is not a knowing experience, according to how the world has taught us to know. It is neither thought nor felt, but experienced through the strange silence of pure *being*. This is the stillness of prayer at its deepest level. "Be still and know that I am God."[71]

The experience feels like nothing, but as we practice it on a regular basis, we notice that we do not worry about what we will eat or what we will drink. As time passes, we notice that wounds that kept us from forgiveness and mercy are no longer there, and that part of us that held those wounds no longer exists. In time, prayer, as the practiced experience of God's presence at the core of our being, is what brings us into that deeper life in God. It is not something we do, but something God does as we give permission to end our life in the world in order that we might enter into the reign of God. Prayer is what brings us to be able to say, "It is no longer I that live, but it is Christ who lives in me."[72]

Prayer is also the place we go in order to receive faith, not as something to know and believe, but something to become. Faith is a being thing and not a knowing thing. Without that level of consciousness that is prayer at its deepest level, we will only hear what conforms to the understanding the world has given us. That understanding will always filter out the words of Jesus, since his are kingdom words and cannot be heard from the perspective of who we have learned to be in the world.

Prayer, as that altered state of consciousness where the world becomes dim so that we might see the beauty and goodness of

---

71. Psalm 46:10.
72. Galatians 2:20.

Jesus' words, is perhaps harder to find today than ever before. Today, mass media, the internet, and our phones constantly connect us to the world. By contrast, prayer is about disconnecting ourselves from that level of consciousness that connects us to the world in order to experience our deeper connection to God. That connection is not established by what we claim to know and believe, but through the raw experience of God's presence at the core of our being.

The modern worlds of both science and religion have denied the existence of such a deeper and more personal reality. To the modern world, only what can be verified by others counts as true. As we have seen, however, objective truth is an illusion that we create out of the dualistic, subject/object perspective of the left-brain. In truth, we all experience the world differently because of the perspective through which we interpret the data of our experience. Certainly, we can find people with similar perspectives and identify with them in order to create the illusion of objective reality, but we have to avoid any broader exposure to people with perspectives different from our own. Of course, the idea of objective truth is valuable as an abstract concept in order to create our maps and theories about the world, but no one has ever experienced objective truth. Our experience is always personal and molded by our perspective. We do not experience objects independent of our interpretation of them. That is the lie of the subject/object perspective. We do not experience objects but phenomena that are a composite of both the thing itself and our perspective or the socio-cultural meaning we attribute to that thing. We never experience anything objectively or without a perspective. The ultimate point of the gospel is about acquiring Jesus' perspective, and not about acquiring objective truths or abstract theories and maps concerning how to get to heaven.

Over the last hundred and fifty years, the development of psychology as a discipline has helped us realize that what is going on inside of us is often more important than what is going on outside of us. Prayer is a matter of taking a break from what is going on around us and allowing God to work on what is going on inside of us. This deeper reality is accessed through the non-dual, unitive consciousness that allows us to experience the indwelling of the Divine presence of which Jesus and the mystics speak. It is not experiencing God as an object but as an indwelling presence, which connects us to God and his creation, rather than the world that human beings have created. Prayer, in its ultimate form is the way we return to our original being in God. The more time we spend experiencing our unitive consciousness and its connection to God and all other human beings, the less time we spend pursuing the world's illusions of happiness.

Jesus constantly says things that make no sense, but that is because he is speaking from that altered state of consciousness to which he is calling us. The more we practice that altered state of consciousness and come to identify with it, the more sense his words make. If we never go to that alternative level of consciousness that is prayer, we will always ignore his words and attach ourselves to doctrines and theologies that offer us ways around his words.

From our place in the world, it makes no sense that God is "kind to the ungrateful and the wicked"?[73] And why is there "more

---

73. Luke 6:35.

joy in heaven over one sinner who repents than over ninety-nine righteous persons who need no repentance?"[74] Why does Jesus tell us to judge no one in order that we will not be judged,[75] and forgive everyone or God will not forgive us.[76] None of these things make any sense from our understanding in the world, so we create doctrines that do make sense, but doctrines never transform us into his likeness. That is something that only his words can do.

Jesus' words can never take root in the person we have created in order to be in the world. That is because, "What is prized by human beings is an abomination in the sight of God."[77] As long as we seek to be who the world tells us to be, we will never take the words of Jesus seriously. The more time we spend in an awareness of the Divine presence at the core of our being, however, the more we begin to identify with God rather than the world, and the more we are able to see the beauty and goodness of Jesus' words and want them for ourselves. Indeed, a daily practice of prayer brings us to that deeper level of being in God rather than being in the world. If we practice it enough, it eventually brings us to a place beneath the kind of knowing the world has given us, and allows for the raw, transformative experience that Jesus' words are intended to produce.

---

74. Luke 15:7.
75. Matthew 7:1-2
76. Matthew 6:15, and Mark 11:26.
77. Luke 16:15.

CHAPTER FIVE

The Parable of the Sower

In all three of the synoptic Gospels, Jesus offers the parable of the sower.

> Listen! A sower went out to sow. And as he sowed, some seeds fell on the path, and the birds came and ate them up. Other seeds fell on rocky ground, where they did not have much soil, and they sprang up quickly, since they had no depth of soil. But when the sun rose, they were scorched; and since they had no root, they withered away. Other seeds fell among thorns, and the thorns grew up and choked them. Other seeds fell on good soil and brought forth grain, some a hundredfold, some sixty, some thirty.[78]

After having heard this, the disciples came to Jesus and asked why Jesus speaks in parables. His answer seems shocking. He says, "the reason I speak to them in parables is that 'seeing they do not perceive, and hearing they do not listen, nor do they understand.'" People do not want stories, they want answers. Jesus seldom gives us answers. In fact, of the almost two hundred questions asked of Jesus throughout the Gospels, he only answers a handful. His usual response to a question is to ask a

---

78. Matthew 13:3-8. Also see Mark 4:1-20, and Luke 8:4-15.

question in return, answer a different question than the one that was asked, or simply remain silent. The mystery that is both God and our relationship to God is not a puzzle to be solved with an answer, but a mystery with ever deeper meaning. Our lives are great stories because there is always more going on in our lives than we are usually aware. Mysteries are not solved but explored. Mystery novels are not really about mysteries, but merely puzzles that have solutions. Divine mysteries do not have solutions, but if we explore them, they reveal beauty, goodness, and truth on ever deeper levels. In the case of the parable above, Jesus does try to help his disciples by explaining the deeper meaning of the parable.

> Hear then the parable of the sower. When anyone hears the word of the kingdom and does not understand it, the evil one comes and snatches away what is sown in the heart; this is what was sown on the path. As for what was sown on rocky ground, this is the one who hears the word and immediately receives it with joy; yet such a person has no root, but endures only for a while, and when trouble or persecution arises on account of the word, that person immediately falls away. As for what was sown among thorns, this is the one who hears the word, but the cares of the world and the lure of wealth choke the word, and it yields nothing. But as for what was sown on good soil, this is the one who hears the word and understands it, who indeed bears fruit and yields, in one case a hundredfold, in another sixty, and in another thirty."[79]

Notice that Jesus is talking about the kingdom and not the world. In order to hear his words we need to identify with who we

---

79. Matthew 13:18-23.

are in his kingdom rather than the person we have created in order to be in the world. Jesus words will never make sense to the person we are in the world. His words are kingdom words and only make sense to those who identify with his kingdom rather than the world. If our identity is in the world, we are living on the path of which Jesus speaks and "the evil one comes and snatches away what is sown in the heart."[80] Those who live on rocky ground hear Jesus' words and receive them but when troubles arise because of his words, they fall away because his words are not rooted in the deep soil of who they are in God. A third group of people are those who hear "the word, but the cares of the world and the lure of wealth choke the word, and it yields nothing."[81] Finally, there are those who hear "the word and understand it"[82], but that understanding is radically different from the understanding that the world has given us. The understanding that is able to receive Jesus' words is the understanding of who we are in God rather than who we are in the world. It is the mystical understanding of our being in God, and God being in us that we have access to through the unitive level of consciousness.

As long as we operate out of the identity and understanding the world has given us, Christians may love the name of Jesus, but the words of Jesus are too strange to be taken seriously by most who consider themselves Christians. Thus, we create churches that love the Bible but avoid the words of Jesus. The popular gospel gives most Christians what they want; which is to avoid hell

---

80. Matthew 13:19.
81. Matthew 13:22.
82. Matthew 13:23.

and gain heaven at the cheapest possible price. If you can throw in health and wealth as well that would be great, but such a gospel has to avoid the words of Jesus, which tell a very different story.

The gospel is two thousand years old. The doctrines and beliefs that constitute today's popular notions of Christianity are the product of the modern world and have to avoid the words of Jesus, which are never compatible with the world, and especially the modern world. If belief in those doctrines is what establishes an individual as a true follower of Jesus, then there were no true followers of Jesus until a few hundred years ago. The truth of the gospel has to be something that runs throughout the history of the church. That is never the case with doctrines and theologies that constantly change to accommodate the vicissitudes of history and our ever changing human understanding. Only the words of Jesus, and the kind of prayer that is able to make sense of those words, represent the gospel at its deepest level.

> With them indeed is fulfilled the prophecy of Isaiah that says: you will indeed listen, but never understand, and you will indeed look, but never perceive. For this people's heart has grown dull, and their ears are hard of hearing, and they have shut their eyes; so that they might not look with their eyes, and listen with their ears, and understand with their hearts and turn – and I would heal them.[83]

Jesus' words are always calling us to repentance, but it is not a repentance of remorse over what Moses told us were our sins, but rather a matter of changing our minds about who we

---

83. Matthew 13:14-15.

are. Our identity in the world is based upon the world's values and our adaptation to them in order to create the false-self, which is our identity in the world. Jesus, however, tells us that God is our Father and we are his beloved daughters and sons. That is not what the world tells us. The world tells us that there are good people and bad people based upon things like ones' reputation, achievements, disposition, failures, beliefs, and a host of other factors and circumstances many of which were beyond our control. Such things constitute our identity in the world, rather than our identity in God.

Of course, Jesus never speaks about our identity being in God rather than in the world. Identity was not a concept that was available in Jesus' day, but it is clearly what determines whether we are open to making Jesus' words our own or not. As long as we identify with the person we are in the world, and we live our lives out of the understanding the world has given us, the words of his kingdom will never take root within us. The understanding we have inherited from the world filters out any ideas that do not conform to it. That is what knowledge does – it filters the data of our experience to distinguish what is true and important from data that is false or superficial. Jesus' words never appear true or important from the perspective of our inherited understanding in the world. In order to hear his words, we need a different identity, or, to use Jesus' words, a different soil that would allow his words to take root.

The words of Jesus are meant for the eternal soil of our souls and not for the illusions and pretenses of the false-self, which we create in order to pursue the world's agendas for happiness. In order to receive Jesus' words they have to penetrate to the core of our being. They simply cannot take root in the person we have created in order to be in the world, as the parable of the sower explains. As long as we identify with who we are in the world, we will always ignore his words and be attracted to doctrines that appeal to the false-self that we and our socio-cultural world have created. By contrast, if we have a daily practice of seeking the silence and stillness of God's presence, we eventually come to love that experience so much that we come to identify with it rather than the world. When we come to identify with who we are in God's presence, we are able to see that the words of Jesus are the most beautiful words ever spoken.

The teachings of Jesus are the basis for a radically different way to be than the way the world has taught us to be. The most radical of these teachings is that the God of the universe is *our* Father and we are his beloved daughters and sons. God, as our Father, is very different from the way we see God from our perspective in the world. From the subject/object perspective of the dualistic mind that the world has given us, we see God as an object to be feared, obeyed, and worshiped through our beliefs and behavior. A father's love, however, is not in response to his child's fear, obedience, and worship. A father loves his child, because the child has the father's DNA, and the father desires that the child would become like the father in character and virtue. That is the basis for the gospel. Jesus tells us how to be in order that we might be like our heavenly Father. We know that God must forgive everyone because Jesus tells us to forgive everyone. We know that God does not judge us because Jesus tells us not to judge anyone, but simply love our sisters and brothers as our Father loves. God may lament the bad choices we make concerning the things we value and pursue, but that does not deter his love, and it should not deter our love for our sisters and brothers.

Jesus' words describe the kind of character and virtue that our heavenly Father desires for his daughters and sons, because they represent God's own character and virtue, which is almost always contrary to the teachings of our earthly fathers. Recall Jesus saying,

> Whoever comes to me and does not hate father and mother, wife and children, brothers and sisters, yes, even life itself cannot be my disciple.[84]

Our attachment to the world and the ways it has taught us to be is what prevents Jesus' words from taking root and molding us into our heavenly Father's likeness rather than the likeness of our earthly fathers. Indeed, Jesus' words can only take root within that deeper self or who we were in God before the world got a hold of us. The more we love the false-self that we are in the world, the less able we are to hear the words of Jesus.

Not being able to hear the words of Jesus is not something that troubles most Christians, since most people's interest in Jesus is simply as a religious belief that they have been told will get their sins forgiven and make them righteous before God. Most who consider themselves Christians are very happy with righteousness as the forgiveness of sins. From the perspective of God as a distant sovereign who desires obedience and punishes disobedience, the ultimate objective is to have our sins forgiven in order to escape God's wrath and punishment. Jesus, teachings are

---

84. Luke 14:26.

not about getting our sins forgiven but about making us into his forgiving, merciful and loving likeness.

The repentance to which Jesus' words are constantly calling us is not repentance over sin, but repentance or changing our minds about who we are. The life to which Jesus calls us may begin with a belief that we have been forgiven, but Jesus' teachings are always about making us into his forgiving likeness, rather than merely extending forgiveness to us because of something we have done or believe. Becoming Jesus' forgiveness to the world requires that we become that special kind of soil that is able to receive his words. In the parable of the sower, the soil that is able to receive Jesus' words is very different from the soil that does not receive his words. The soil that receives Jesus' word is a metaphor for that different level of consciousness that is able to see how beautiful and good his words are. This is why prayer, as a different level of consciousness, is so important. It is only from our original, unitive consciousness that we can love our neighbor as ourselves. Loving our neighbor as ourselves is impossible from the subject/object perspective of the left-brain. The mind we inherit from the world is the dualist mind that puts our interests above the interests of others. That is part of the survival instinct that comes with our being in the world. That is not the mind that Jesus' words address, except when he is speaking to the religious leaders of his day. When speaking to his disciples, Jesus words address that unitive level of consciousness that sees oneself in one's neighbor and even one's enemy. That is the heavenly level of consciousness to which Jesus' words call us.

His are living words. They are not words to know and believe but words to become. As such, they can never take root in the person that the world has created but only in the person that God has created. Our soul is God's creation and our connection to God, but the world is very good at distracting us from that deeper life in God. As long as our identity is grounded in this world rather than in God, we will always avoid the words of Jesus, simply because they make no sense from our perspective in the world. Who we are in the world can act religiously, and use the name of Jesus, but his words can only take root in the rich soil of our soul, or who we were in God before the world got a hold of us and began making us into its likeness.

As long as we identify with who we are in the world, rather than who we are in God, we can love Jesus as our savior, but we cannot see beyond that from our perspective in the world. Jesus' words are communicated on a different frequency to which only our soul has access. Our soul, or whatever word you want to use for that deepest part of you that is God's creation rather than who you and the world have created, is the only part of you that can hear Jesus tells us to not respond to violence with violence[85] and to love even our enemies.[86]

The words of Jesus cannot be contained in the old wineskin, which is the mind the world has given us. The intoxicating new wine of Jesus' words has little or no effect upon the person we are in the world. His words are intended for the rich soil of our soul, or that part of us which connects us to both God and every other human being. His words will always burst the old wineskin, which is the left-brain's understanding that we have inherited from the

---

85. Matthew 5:38-39.
86. Matthew 5:43-45.

world. Only the silence and stillness of prayer allows us to get to that core of our being and the unitive consciousness that is able to hear the words of Jesus. Unless we have a daily practice of tending the soil of our soul in order to receive Jesus' words, the world and all of its concerns will consume us.

The silence and stillness of prayer is the way we prepare the soil of our soul to receive Jesus' words, and without that alternative level of consciousness that is prayer, at its deepest level, Jesus' words will never take root within us. The life to which Jesus calls us is radically different from our life in the world, and it requires a different mind or level of consciousness than the mind and level of consciousness that the world has given us. Prayer, at its deepest level, is the way we practice detaching from the world, in order to hear the words of Jesus. It is our dying to the false-self and all of the demands the world places upon that self, in order that we might be in the world, but no longer of the world. Prayer, in its ultimate form, is about our own death and resurrection. Death and resurrection is not just about Jesus but about us as well. The only way into the fullness of life is through death.

> For those who want to save their life will lose it, and those who lose their life for my sake, and for the sake of the gospel, will save it. For what will it profit them to gain the whole world and forfeit their life?[87]

The popular notion of the gospel tells us that the new life that Jesus offers is free and comes at the cost of a mere belief. Jesus, however, tells us that the fullness of life comes only through the

---

87. Mark 8:35; also see Matthew 10:39, 16:25. Luke` 9:24.

death of who we are in the world. That death is much easier for the poor, powerless, and infamous, than it is for the rich, powerful, and famous. This is why Jesus says that he came "to bring good news to the poor,"[88] since it is much easier for them to relinquish their identity in the world.

Of course, our initial notion of the gospel usually comes to us through the voices of the rich, powerful, and famous. They represented the hierarchy of the church in the past, and today are the celebrity Christians who have access to television and book deals with larger publishers. Some Christians even go so far as to claim that their wealth, power, and prestige are the result of their relationship with Jesus, and they claim it can be the result of our relationship with Jesus as well. The only requirement is that we ignore the words of Jesus, which always call us to a deeper life than one of pursuing the world's programs for happiness. True, there may be a place for such a gospel but it is a starting place and not a place that leads to the fullness of life of which Jesus speaks. Jesus calls us to a spiritual journey – a *Pilgrim's Progress* – but we all get to choose how far we want to go. We may start with the popular gospel that tells us that God wants to give us his forgiveness through Jesus' sacrificial death. The gospel of Jesus' words, however, tells us that God wants us to become his forgiveness and mercy to the world. That is a deeper level of truth and it requires a deeper level of consciousness and identity. It is not the truth of an epistemic belief that we have been forgiven, but the ontological truth that we want to become like Jesus in order to be God's forgiveness and mercy to the world. This deeper life to which Jesus

---

88. Luke 4:18.

is always calling us is about the truth of who God made us to be, rather than merely the epistemic truth of what we claim to believe in order to be saved from God's wrath.

From the perspective of the popular gospel, repentance is a onetime event for the remission of sins. From the perspective of who we are in God, repentance is a constant changing of our minds every time we find ourselves identifying with who we are in the world, rather than identifying with our deeper life in God. The life to which Jesus calls us is one of constant repentance for believing that we are who the world tells us we are, rather than who Jesus tells us we are. Jesus tells us that the God of the universe is our Father and we are all his daughters and sons. This is not something to know and believe along with all of the other things that we know and believe. It is not intended to be part of our knowing and believing but part of our eternal being. Many people claim to know and believe in Jesus. They even profess to do great works in Jesus' name, but Jesus has amazing things to say about that.

> On that day, many will say to me, 'Lord, Lord, did we not prophesy in your name, and cast out demons in your name, and do many deeds of power in your name?' Then I will declare to them, 'I never knew you; go away from me, you evildoers.'[89]

Notice that he does not say that they never knew him, but that *he* never knew them. What is that supposed to mean? We think that it is about us knowing Jesus, but Jesus says it is about him knowing us, and placing his seed, which is his word, at the core of our

---

89. Matthew 7:22-23.

being. This is the kind of knowing of which the Bible speaks when it tells us, "Now the man knew his wife Eve, and she conceived and bore Cain."[90] It is that deeper knowing that is done to us in order to create new life. The knowing that *we* do is epistemic; the knowing that God does is ontological and able to create our eternal being in Jesus' likeness rather than the likeness of the world. In the world, we want to know, but the life to which Jesus calls us is not about our knowing, but about our allowing Jesus to know us and plant the seed of his word at the deepest core of our being.

Jesus' words are the most counter-cultural words ever spoken. He tells us that we are not to resist evil but merely suffer it and offer the other cheek to be struck as well.[91] He tells us to love our enemies and pray for those that persecute us.[92] He tells us not to pray in public or even use words when we pray, because God already knows what our needs are.[93] What are we supposed to do with the fact that Jesus tells us that he did not "come to abolish the law or the prophets"[94], and then he gives us six examples of what he says in contrast to what the law had said?[95] How are we to understand the strange things that Jesus says?

The choice is quite simple, and one that Christians have had to make for two thousand years. Either we ignore the words of Jesus, and find a version of the gospel that offers a way around his words, or we find that deeper level of consciousness from which we can see the beauty and goodness of his words and make them

90. Genesis 4:1.
91. Matthew 5:39.
92. Matthew 5:44.
93. Matthew 6:8.
94. Matthew 5:17.
95. Matthew 5:17-48.

our own. His words are not like the words that constitute our religious doctrines and theologies. His words are the seeds of eternal life that produce the ontological truth of who God made us to be, but they cannot take root in the person that we have created. They can only take root in the deep soil of our soul or who we were in God before the world got a hold of us.

Of course, building our life upon his words has never been the popular solution. The popular notion of the gospel always offers something much more attractive. Those who are content with their live in the world do not want transformation into a radically different way to be, but merely want to be assured of a heavenly afterlife. Thus, religions that offer the assurance of heaven in exchange for an epistemic belief, rather than a transformation into an entirely different way to be, are enormously attractive.

The Jesus of the popular gospel is a savior who pays for our sins and thus makes us righteous before God. By contrast, the Jesus of the Gospels is not interested in forgiving us. He is interested in making us into his forgiving likeness in order that we might experience the fullness of life. From our perspective in the world, forgiveness is something to receive, but from our perspective in God, forgiveness is one of the things that release us from our attachment to the world, and all of the wounds that the world has inflicted upon us.

Jesus did not preach a gospel of salvation through God's forgiveness of our sins. Jesus preached the fullness of life through our forgiveness of others. God never had a problem forgiving us, although as long as we have a problem with forgiving others, we will imagine a god that is like us regarding forgiveness and love. We will insist that God demands payment for our sins because we demand payment from those who have sinned against us. Our forgiveness of others, however, is what releases the hold the world has upon us and allows us to come into the fullness of life to which Jesus calls us. The wounds that we received, beginning in childhood and continuing throughout our lives, are what shape the person we become in the world. Only forgiveness releases us from those wounds. The problem is not a matter of getting God to forgive us – God is good at forgiveness, as Jesus reveals in forgiving his torturers from the Cross. "Father, forgive them; for they do not know what they are doing."[96] The problem is not a matter of getting God to forgive us but a matter of us forgiving those who have sinned against us. We are the ones that have a problem with forgiveness and in the early stages of the spiritual journey we transfer our own lack of forgiveness onto God. Time in God presence and Jesus' words are the only things that can bring us to that deeper repentance. The deeper repentance that Jesus calls us to is not repentance over our sins, but repentance or changing our minds about those who have sinned against us. Jesus says,

> For if you forgive others their trespasses, your heavenly Father will also forgive you; but if you do not forgive others, neither will your Father forgive your trespasses.[97]

Holding unforgiveness is the great sin of religious people, who want to be forgiven because of something righteous they have done, but do not want to extend forgiveness to others who have not met their righteous standard for forgiveness. Forgiveness,

---

96. Luke 23:34.
97. Matthew 6:14-15.

however, is not something to receive but something to give away in order to be free. Unforgiveness is the great sin that keeps us from the deeper life to which Jesus calls us. Likewise, it is not something that God can forgive because it is not something that we have done, but something that we refuse to do.

When we begin a relationship with God, it is easy to imagine that God must be like us and demand payment for our sins, just as we demand payment from those who have sinned against us. This is why Jesus' words are so important, since they reveal that God is nothing like us, and calls us to be radically different from the person that the world has made us to be. Jesus tells us that our heavenly Father "is kind to the ungrateful and the wicked"[98], and we should "be merciful, just as your Father is merciful."[99] Becoming merciful, like becoming forgiving, is what releases the hold the world has upon us and allows us to become God's love to the world. Mercy is the lack of judgment that allows us to freely love as God loves. Forgiveness and mercy are what keep God's love flowing through us, and unforgiveness and judgment are what stop that flow. Forgiveness and mercy are the divine virtues that are so contrary to the world's virtues that they require an entirely different way of being than the way the world has taught us to be. This is why Jesus tells us that we cannot even see the kingdom of which he speaks without being born from above. "Very truly, I tell you, no one can see the kingdom of God without being born from above."[100] Seeing the kingdom of God requires a perspective that

---

98. Luke 6:35.
99. Luke 6:36.
100.   John 3:3.

is very different from our perspective in the world. As we have seen, in the world, we operate out of the subject/object perspective that is appropriate to our being in the world, but Jesus calls us to a radically different way of being in God rather than being in the world. Our being in God requires that unitive consciousness that we share with God and all other human beings. That alone gives us the perspective from which to see the beauty and goodness of Jesus' words, and without that perspective we will always create doctrines and theologies that attempt to get around his words.

The gospel, at its deepest level of meaning, is about the mystery of our transformation into Jesus' likeness, but this level of meaning cannot be accessed through our normal level of consciousness that connects us to the world. For this deeper life to which Jesus calls us, we need that deeper level of consciousness that connects us to God and all other human beings. God has certainly equipped us with such a level of consciousness, although it had been largely suppressed by the scientific, religious, and economic thinking of modernity. Fortunately, our recent history has brought us to see the shallowness of such thinking. Just when it appeared that the mystery that enraptured the medieval mystics had been eclipsed by the modern mind and its thinking, God allowed us to see a little deeper into the nature of the bicameral brain and its receptivity to different levels of consciousness.

What the parable of the sower reveals is that Jesus' words cannot take root in the understanding that the world has given us. His are kingdom words and they can only take root in our identity in God rather than who we are in the world. From our perspective in the world, his words will be snatched away, because we are either living too close to the path that the world has provided for us,[101] or his words will fail to take root because they create trouble for who we are in the world.[102] "As for what was sown among thorns, this is the one who hears the word, but the cares of the world and the lure of wealth choke the word, and it yields nothing."[103] So in spite of what Jesus says about how difficult it is for his words to take root within us, how did Christianity ever become the most popular religion in the world?

101.   Ibid.
102.   Matthew 13:20-21.
103.   Matthew 13:22.

CHAPTER SIX

Christianity Lite

The marketing of Christianity is probably as old as Christianity itself. There has always been a "Christianity Lite", which avoids the words of Jesus and offers ways around them. Even before Constantine became a Christian because he believed Jesus gave him a way to win battles, there were those who wanted the power of Jesus name but not his words. It is as if his words are only for his disciples, but the church will always find ways to offer a popular version of the gospel to those who want enough of Jesus to feel righteous about themselves, but not so much of Jesus that it would put them at odds with the world. Therefore, the more popular forms of Christianity avoid the words of Jesus and offer a version of the gospel that is more compatible with the world. Today, the way this is accomplished is by making the Bible the word of God, rather than Jesus being the word of God. The Bible, however, nowhere claims to be the word of God, but it does claim that Jesus is the word of God.

> In the beginning was the Word and the Word was with God, and the Word was God. He was in the beginning with God.

All things came into being through him, and without him not
one thing came into being.[104]

The book of Revelation also attests that, "his name is called
the Word of God."[105] True, the Bible is God's revelation of human
beings' relationship with God. As such, however, it reveals human
beings' experiences with God from a variety of socio-cultural perspectives. Remember, objectivity is an abstract idea created by
the subject/object perspective and not something that anyone ever
experiences. The world of our experience is a phenomenal world
that is a composite of both the things we experience and the way
we have been taught to interpret those things. There are no un-in-
terpreted experiences except for the ineffable experience of God's
indwelling presence that we are able to experience in prayer.

Experiencing God's indwelling presence is achieved through
detachment from the world. God is omnipresent but we can only
experience that presence when we are present. In our normal state
of consciousness we are rarely present, because the world and
its concerns keep us constantly distracted from an awareness of
God's presence. Our minds are constantly flooded with thought
after thought. The silence of prayer is the only place of escape
from the world and all of the thoughts that keep us connected to
the world. As we have said, this silent place of prayer is not an
easy place to find, but God "rewards those that seek him."[106] The
reward for seeking God's presence is that it gets us to a place from
which we can identify with our original being in God rather than

---

104.   John 1:1-3.
105.   Revelation 19:13.
106.   Hebrews 11:6.

the world, and it is only from that place that we can see the beauty and goodness of Jesus' words.

> Blessed are you when people revile you and persecute you and utter all kinds of evil against you falsely on my account. Rejoice and be glad, for your reward is great in heaven, for in the same way they persecuted the prophets who were before you.[107]

From our perspective in the world, it is not good to be reviled and persecuted. This, like all of Jesus' words to his disciples, represents a very different perspective than the perspective the world has given us. Jesus' words provide us with a heavenly perspective that most of us are not ready for, so the popular gospel of Christianity Lite offers a way around the hard words of Jesus. It claims that the entire Bible is the objective revelation of God's nature, so if Jesus says things that do not make sense, we can find other places in scripture that do make sense. Thus, we can build our life in God upon whatever portion of the Bible we are comfortable with, since the entire Bible is revealing the same objective nature of God.

In truth, however, the experiences that are recorded in the Bible are experiences of God from a vast variety of socio-cultural perspectives, while Jesus' experiences of God are from the perspective of a Son to a Father. We, however, are much more comfortable with the more human and less divine perspectives that we find in the Bible rather than the Gospels. We find it much easier to identify with the human interpretations throughout the

---

107.   Matthew 5:11-12.

Bible rather than the Divine interpretation offered by Jesus. No one prior to Jesus had the perspective that the God of the universe was "our Father." When we change our perspective and accept Jesus' perspective of God as "our Father" everything changes. God is no longer a distant sovereign who demands obedience and punishes disobedience, but a loving Father who desires his daughters and sons to be like "our Father" in terms of character and virtue. Of course, if we have not gone very far in the spiritual journey to which Jesus calls us, we much prefer a distant God who demands nothing but obedience and worship, rather than a Father/God who desires his children to be like the Divine in character and virtue.

Early on in the spiritual journey we much prefer the capricious God of the Bible to the Father/God that Jesus reveals. A capricious God who sometimes loves his enemies and "is kind to the ungrateful and the wicked,"[108] but at other times wants us to kill the babies in Jericho[109] can be an attractive God. Indeed, if God is sometimes merciful and sometimes wrathful, that gives us the option to decide whether the situation in which we find ourselves is one that calls for mercy or wrath. This is why we love the Bible. It gives us options to justify almost anything we want to do, while Jesus' words take away those options and calls us to a constant state of repentance for not being God's forgiveness and mercy to the world. I have heard people boast that they believe in the "entire Bible and not just the words of Jesus," as if that were revealing more of God rather than less. We want to interpret Jesus

---

108.   Luke 6:35.
109.   Joshua 6:21.

in the context of the rest of the Bible, rather than interpreting the rest of the Bible through the words of Jesus. We want Jesus to be our Savior, who pays for our sins, but has nothing to say about our character and virtues. What is so attractive about a gospel stripped of Jesus' words is that it equates righteousness with being forgiven rather than with becoming forgiving.

The popular form of Christianity Lite claims that Jesus is the Messiah, the ultimate blood sacrifice who takes away our sins. Jesus is the scape goat[110] upon whom we place our sins in order to become sinless. Furthermore, all we need to do is accept the epistemic belief that Jesus suffered the penalty of our sin in our place, and we are therefore made sinless and righteous before God through our belief. Christianity Lite equates the forgiveness of sins with righteousness, and even adds that there is nothing we can do to add to our righteousness apart from Jesus redeeming work on the Cross, which neatly negates all the words of Jesus. What a neat trick to undermine the words of Jesus and the deeper life to which his words call us. From our perspective in the world, such a doctrine does sound like good news, especially to people who love their lives in this world and hate the things that Jesus has to say about people who love their lives in this world.

> Those who love their life lose it, and those who hate their life in this world will keep it for eternal life. Whoever serves me must follow me, and where I am, there my servant will be also.[111]

---

110. Leviticus 16:1-34.
111. John 12:25-26.

If we love the world and our place in it, we want the gospel to end with the forgiveness of our sins. That, however, requires that we avoid the words of Jesus which are always calling us to become Jesus' forgiveness to the world. Becoming Jesus' forgiveness to the world is the ontological truth of the Gospels, rather than the epistemic truth of Christianity Lite. As we have seen, truth as something to believe is very different from truth as something to be. God is interested in our being, and not in the concocted beliefs we attach ourselves to in order to feel righteous. We are not made into his likeness by the things we believe, but by making his words our own. Our beliefs are part of our left-brain's understanding that attaches us to the world; Jesus' words attach us to his kingdom and are always addressing our being and not merely our beliefs.

The Gospels are not about God meeting human beings in the world and those individuals interpreting that encounter out of their culturally inherited understanding, as is the case with most of the Bible. Jesus is speaking out of a perspective, which is nothing like the cultural perspective with which the world has equipped us. His words cannot be interpreted from our inherited, cultural understanding. His words are addressing who we are in God and not who we are in the world. Our left-brain's inherited cultural understanding cannot hear Jesus' words because, "the cares of the world and the lure of wealth choke the word, and it yields nothing."[112]

The words of Jesus, when taken seriously, always put us at odds with the world. Christianity Lite is for people who like their life in world but want just enough of Jesus to assure them of eternal

---

112.   Matthew 13:22

life, but not so much of Jesus that it would be disruptive to their life in the world. Religions based upon beliefs in epistemic truths, rather than the ontological truth of Jesus' words which address our being rather than our beliefs, are very popular. Indeed, they have created over forty thousand Christian denominations world-wide, but they must avoid the hard words of Jesus which are always addressing our being rather than what we believe. Jesus' words are always calling us to repentance not for some sin that we have committed but repentance or changing our minds about who we are. His words describe a radically different way to be than the way the world has taught us to be. You may have a belief that you have been forgiven, but you cannot become forgiving through a belief. That requires a living transformation into the truth of the person to whom Jesus is calling us to be.

A belief that we have been forgiven is much more appealing than becoming forgiving. Everyone wants to be forgiven, but few want to become the agents of forgiveness. Christianity Lite is perfect for those who want forgiveness as something to receive through a belief rather than a radical transformation into a new kind of forgiving being. Christianity Lite allows us to think of ourselves as righteous rather than being in a constant state of repentance over Jesus' words and the unsettling transformation they produce when taken seriously.

With Christianity Lite, the born again experience is a new belief, rather than that new state of being *in* God rather than being *in* the world. The born again experience is meant to take place at the deepest level of our being and not in what we know and believe. It requires not only a new birth but the death of who we are in the world in order that who Jesus is calling us to be might come forth. The gospel is not about getting us saved from God's wrath, but about getting us transformed from who we are in the world to who we are in God. This is the nature of the spiritual journey to which Jesus calls us.

The righteousness of Christianity Lite is based upon a theory that Jesus suffered God's wrath in our place, and since our sins have been paid for, we are now righteous before God. That makes sense if your subject/object perspective of God is that of a distant sovereign who rewards obedience and punishes disobedience, but, as we have said, the most important thing that Jesus ever said was "our Father."[113] Indeed, if God is really our Father, God wants what all good fathers want, which is not simply obedience but that their children would be like them in terms of character and virtue. That is what the older brother in the story of the prodigal never gets. He wants his obedience for not sinning to be rewarded, but he is not interested in becoming like his father in terms of forgiveness and mercy.

Of course, when we are young, it is easy to think that our earthly father's only desire our obedience, and with some earthly fathers that might be the extent of their interest. The best of fathers, however, direct us in order that we would become like them in character and virtue. That is certainly the case with our heavenly Father, although the kind of character and virtue that Jesus tells us our heavenly Father wants to produce within us is nothing like what the world tells us will make us happy. Jesus is always addressing our eternal happiness and not the illusions of happiness that the world sets before us. Of course, for people

---

113.   Matthew 6:9 et al.

who identify with who they are in the world, such illusions appear very attractive. It is very easy to recruit such people to Christian churches simply by playing down the actual teachings of Jesus and reducing Jesus to a savior who pays for our sins, but has nothing important to say that is different from everything that has already been said in the Bible.

When we take Jesus' words seriously, however, and believe that God is our Father, we realize that our Father's desire is to make us into his forgiving and merciful likeness. Of course, if we had a terrible human father whose ego was offended through our disobedience, we might imagine God to be a similar father. Great fathers, however, have no egos when it comes to their children's welfare. Their only care is for their child and their desire for the child to realize the fullness of life. Jesus reveals that fullness of life and the ultimate nature of God, or as much of God as we can know, because he is the perfect son who reflects his Father's nature.

The experience of God as our Father is radically different from the knowledge of God as an object of reverence and worship. Some never venture beyond that notion of God that we have from the subject/object perspective that the world has given us. From that perspective, God is yet another object that we encounter in life and need to find our way around. Christianity Lite tells us how to do that by getting our sins forgiven in order that we might be righteous before God. From the unitive level of consciousness that experiences God as both our Father and an indwelling presence, however, we no longer equate righteousness with the forgiveness of sins, but with the heavenly virtues of Jesus' teachings. Jesus' notion of God as "our Father" puts everything in a different light.

From the subject/object perspective of who we are in the world, we fear that God might not forgive us, but from the unitive perspective of God as our Father our fear is that we might not live up to God's hope for us.

I once had a student tell me that when he was young, he avoided doing wrong things because he feared that his father would punish him. When he got older, he always sought to do the right thing because he feared that not doing so would hurt his father. This is the progression of the spiritual life. It is not a matter of going from the beliefs that the world gave us, to new beliefs about God, but about coming into the ontological truth of who "our Father" desires us to be. That is the great revelation of the Gospels. By telling us how we should be; Jesus is telling us the nature of our Father/God who desires us to be like the Divine.

Our experience of God as our Father is what gives us access to Jesus' words, but it also conversely puts us at odds with the world, and especially the world of formal religion. The more Jesus' perspective becomes our own, the more heretical we will appear to Christianity Lite in whatever age we happen to find ourselves. Both Teresa of Avila (1515-1582) and John of the Cross (1542-1591) were under constant threat from the Spanish Inquisition. Today, we don't threaten heretics with torture or being burned alive, but people who take Jesus too seriously are often not welcomed by people whose faith is in their doctrinal beliefs rather than the transformative words of Jesus. Jesus' words are heretical to most popular forms of Christianity, since the basis for most forms of Christianity is our inherited cultural understanding. Today, we would be hard pressed to find any teachings of Jesus that are compatible with the understanding which we have inherited from our contemporary world. Christianity Lite is usually quick to agree with that statement, and argue that liberals have made our culture into something ungodly, but in truth, many agnostics and atheists live closer to the teachings of Jesus than many Bible believing Christians.

Of course, Christianity Lite tells us that the essence of the gospel is not about the teachings of Jesus, but about his death and resurrection as payment for our sin. The great mystery of the Cross is part of the mystery of God and our relationship with God. To reduce that mystery to a propitiation theory of atonement concocted by an eleventh century Archbishop of Canterbury about Jesus suffering God's wrath in our place is to trivialize the cosmic meaning of the Cross. Twenty-first century science has brought us to understand that the physical universe itself is more of a mystery than previous generations could have imagined. The same can be said of its Creator. As we have repeatedly said, God is forever beyond our knowing but not beyond our experience.

Knowing is one of the great illusions the world places before us. The science and philosophy of every generation believes that they have finally discovered the truth that explains the mystery. Trusting what our left-brain is able to know is what ends the spiritual journey into ever deeper life and meaning. Claiming to know God, and claiming to know what happened on that Cross, works as long as we keep God at a distance. If God is a distant sovereign who demands obedience and punishes disobedience, then God torturing Jesus for our sin makes sense. When we draw close, however, and experience God as the loving Father that Jesus words explain, the mystery of the Cross becomes something for us to experience, rather than a doctrine to believe. Jesus never gives us a formula for salvation; he simply says "follow me"[114] seventeen times throughout the Gospels. Five of those times he tells us to pick up our cross and follow him.

> He called the crowd with his disciples, and said to them, "If any want to become my followers, let them deny themselves and take up their cross and follow me. For those who want to save their life will lose it, and those who lose their life for my sake, and the sake of the gospel, will save it. For what will it profit them to gain the whole world and forfeit their life? Indeed, what can they give in return for their life? Those who are ashamed of me and of my words in this adulterous and sinful generation, of them the Son of Man will be ashamed when he comes in the glory of his Father with the holy angels."[115]

Jesus death on the Cross is so much more than Jesus paying for our sins. You may start the spiritual journey there, but the Cross and its ultimate meaning goes way beyond what we can think or imagine. The Cross is not something to know along with everything else we claim to know, but something to behold as an experience whose meaning we will spend eternity exploring. God has placed us in the midst of a great mystery, and every time we think we have figured it out, God reveals a little more of just how mysterious it all is. Jesus is not a theologian that explains the nature of God, which is beyond our understanding, but not beyond our experience. Jesus simply tells us how to be in relationship to

---

114.   Matthew 4:19; 8:22; 9:9; 16:24; 19:21; Mark 2:14; 8:34; 10:21; Luke 5:27; 9:23, 59; 18:22; John 1:43; 10:27; 12:26; 13:36; 21:19.

115.   Mark 8:34-38.

34-38. Also see, Matthew 10:38-39, 16:24-26; Luke 9:23-26, 14:27.

God and one another. It is not about knowing the gospel but about being the gospel because Jesus' words have taken root at the core of our being. Knowing is that left-brain activity that connects us to the world; being is that deeper level of consciousness that connects us to God and all other human beings. We only get to that deeper level of consciousness by repenting for who we are in the world, and returning to who we were in God before the world got a hold of us and began making us into its likeness.

The will of our Father/God is that we would become the daughters and sons of God not as a belief we proclaim, but as a life we live because Jesus' words have taken root at the core of our being. "Heaven and earth will pass away, but my words will not pass away."[116] His words are the words of eternal life and the basis for the spiritual journey to which he calls us. He says, "If you abide in me, and my words abide in you, ask for whatever you wish, and it will be done for you."[117] Of course, we have all experienced asking and not receiving, because his words do not abide in us. If his words did abide in us, we would not be asking for the foolish things we ask in order to enhance our life in the world rather than our life in God.

All this is not to say that Christianity Lite is a false gospel – it is just an elementary gospel. Long before we can experience the deeper things to which Jesus' words call us, most of us begin with an understanding of the gospel that makes sense from our perspective in the world. The problem with Christianity Lite is that it can give believers a sense of righteousness which prevents them from

---

116.   Matthew 24:35.
117.   John 15:7.

hearing the words of Jesus, and his constant call to repentance or changing our minds about who we are. Being righteous in terms of being forgiven is what ends the spiritual journey of transformation to which Jesus calls us. Repentance or changing our minds about who we are at ever deeper levels is what opens us to the words of Jesus.

Jesus tells us that our need for repentance and the transformative experience of God's forgiveness and mercy is much more than we imagine. This is what Jesus means when he says that he did not come for the righteous but for sinners,[118] or people who were open to ever deeper repentance in order to become ever more like our heavenly Father, whose character and virtue Jesus reveals. The Jesus revelation is the revelation of what God's son would look like in human form, and Jesus' words are telling us how to be those sons or daughters. Most people, however, do not want that much God and that much gospel. Most of us want to know how to get to heaven without it upsetting our lives in the world. Christianity Lite gives people just what they want; Jesus never does. Jesus did not come to teach us the right things to believe but the right way to be, and that can only come through a spiritual journey of repentance in response to his words. He does not tell us how to become forgiven, but how to become forgiving. Christianity Lite offers us beliefs by which we claim to have been forgiven; Jesus' words offer us a path to become his forgiveness to the world.

As we saw with the parable of the sower, Jesus' words cannot take root in the person we are in the world. Our left-brain's

---

118.   Matthew 9:13; Mark 2:17; Luke 5:32.

understanding, which the world has given us, is quick to filter out the words of Jesus. That is why we need to access a different level of consciousness in order to hear his words. His words are the words of life, but they are very different than the life the world has equipped us to know. His words are nothing like the maps, theories, and doctrines the world constructs to expedite our life in the world. His words are living words meant to take root and produce fruit. His words are not things to believe but things to become, and, as we have said, they cannot take root in our knowing mind, but require the deep soil of our soul. Our doctrines claim to tell us how to go to heaven, because that is usually all we want to know; but Jesus' words tell us how to be, and therefore, how to bring heaven down to earth.

God is always calling us to a more intimate relationship than the relationship we have with the world. We experience the world through the subject/object perspective, and from that perspective, God is seen as the ultimate object to be feared, obeyed, and worshipped. If, however, we seek to experience God, and identify with that experience the way Jesus did, our understanding of God becomes that of a loving Father, rather than a distant sovereign who responds to us according to our obedience or disobedience. A parent's love is not contingent upon obedience or disobedience, although in our immaturity it may often appear that way. The connection between a parent and a child is that they share the same DNA. We have been made in God's own likeness, but we have also been made free, and we get to choose how much of that likeness, we make our own. We are made into our Father's likeness by allowing Jesus' words to become the basis for our being. From our perspective in the world, however, very little of what Jesus

actually says makes sense. Fortunately, human beings have access
to multiple levels of consciousness and perspectives. The perspective of prayer is that level of our unitive consciousness that gives
us access to God as our Father and the indwelling of his Spirit
at the core of our being. From that perspective and level of consciousness, our sins are not what raise God's ire, but what keep us
from the fullness of life in God.

The fullness of life to which Jesus calls us requires a constant
state of repentance. That is because, according to Jesus, our sin is
our attachment to the world and its programs for happiness, which
keep us from realizing the ultimate happiness and fullness of life
to which God calls us. Worry is a sin, not because it is some sin-
ister evil that will destroy human society, but because it keeps us
from the fullness of life to which Jesus calls us. Worry is actually
something of a virtue in the world, in that it makes us responsible,
but Jesus is talking about our ultimate happiness in God, which
comes through a faith in the fullness of a life that is surrendered to
God and God's provision.

> Therefore I tell you, do not worry about your life, what you
> will eat or what you will drink, or about your body, what
> you will wear. Is not life more than food, and the body more
> than clothing? Look at the birds of the air; they neither sow
> nor reap nor gather into barns, and yet your heavenly Father
> feeds them. Are you not more valuable than they? And can
> any of you by worrying add a single hour to your span of life?
> And why do you worry about clothing? Consider the lilies of
> the field, how they grow; they neither toil nor spin, yet I tell
> you, even Solomon in all his glory was not clothed like one
> of these. But if God so clothes the grass of the field, which is

alive today, and tomorrow is thrown into the oven, will he not much more clothe you—you of little faith?[119]

Worry has nothing to do with the concept of sin that we inherit from our socio-cultural world. When Jesus tells us not to worry, he is speaking of sin in a totally different context. To Jesus, sin is not something to be avoided in order to escape punishment, but what we need to change our mind about in order to realize the fullness of life in God. All of Jesus' teachings are about the fullness of life and not the avoidance of Divine punishment. We almost all start with the concept of God that the world has given us, which uses God as the ultimate enforcer of our tribal laws. The only thing that gets us beyond that tribal god that we inherit from being in the world are the words of Jesus and the time in prayer that is necessary to make sense of those words. God's ultimate desire is to make us into God's own likeness, but we all get to choose how much of that divine likeness we incorporate into our eternal being. We have all been given the freedom to decide how far we want to go with Jesus by choosing how much of his word we make our own.

---

119.   Matthew 6:25-30.

CHAPTER SEVEN

The Words of Jesus and the Fullness of Life

Jesus' words and the prayerful experience of God as a loving Father puts sin in a very different light. Sin to a loving father is what keeps his child from the fullness of life and the true happiness that a divine parent desires for their child. When God is a distant sovereign who demands obedience, and punishes disobedience to God's law, sin is something to be avoided out of fear of punishment. When we experience God as a loving Father, however, sin is what keeps us from the fullness of life that *our Father* desires for us. Thus, repentance is not about remorse over disobedience, but the willingness to change in order to become ever more like our heavenly Father by making Jesus' words our own.

How often have you repented over worry,[120] unforgiveness,[121] judging others,[122] pledging your allegiance to things,[123] responding to violence with violence,[124] not loving your enemies,[125] giving

---

120.   Matthew 6:25-34.
121.   Matthew 6:15, and Mark 11:26.
122.   Matthew 7:1-2
123.   Matthew 5:33-37.
124.   Matthew 5:38-39.
125.   Matthew 5:44-45.

in order to get something in return,[126] loving yourself more than your neighbor,[127] desiring sacrifice rather than mercy,[128] or not giving all of your possessions to the poor?[129] We live according to the world's notion of sin, because Jesus' notion of sin is too strange and upsetting to our life in the world. We much prefer the Bible with Jesus' words removed, because we seek righteousness rather than repentance. The spiritual journey to which Jesus calls us, however, is one of seeing our sin, and need for repentance, on ever deeper levels in order to be the constant recipients of God's transformative forgiveness and mercy.

God does not desire obedience; just as any truly good parent does not simply desire obedience. As a loving Father, the only thing that God desires is our happiness, which God knows can only be found in God rather than in the world. Thus, the repentance to which Jesus calls us is not repentance for what the world tells us are our sins, but repentance or changing our minds about our identity and what will make us happy. The world tells us that things like wealth, power, and prestige, will give us access to the pleasure, fulfillment, and the happiness we desire. Becoming more is the world's prescription for happiness. Jesus' words, however, call us in the opposite direction of becoming less in order to be reduced to love. The way that happens is by paying attention to Jesus' words, which constantly reveal our sin, and need for forgiveness and mercy at ever deeper levels in order that we might love much for having been forgiven much. That is why Jesus tells

---

126.   Luke 14:12-14.
127.   Mark 12:31.
128.   Matthew 9:13, 12:7.
129.   Luke 18:22.

us that "the one to whom little is forgiven, loves little."[130]

Forgiveness is the experience of being loved in spite of our failings. The more we experience it, the more we are able to love others who are in the midst of their failures. Without the constant experience of God's forgiveness for our failure to live by Jesus' words, we can become people who equate being forgiven with righteousness. The forgiveness of sins, however, is not intended to make us righteous; the forgiveness of sins is intended to make us forgiving. The ultimate point of following Jesus is to pay attention to his words in order to see our sin and need for repentance at ever deeper levels in order to be transformed into God's forgiving likeness by having been forgiven much. The experience of being loved in the midst of our sin, rather than in response to our righteousness, is what transforms us into Jesus likeness.

By contrast, religions that preach righteousness through the elimination of sin are very attractive to the false self, but they have to avoid the words of Jesus, which constantly call us to repentance for being who we are in the world rather than who we are in God. Repentance or changing our minds about who we are in response to Jesus' words is what the spiritual journey is all about. We do not become righteous through the forgiveness of sins. We become righteous by becoming forgiving and merciful, for having received much forgiveness and mercy.

As we have seen, the popular gospel tells us that we are made right with God through God's forgiveness in response to our right religious beliefs, but God's forgiveness is not a reaction to our beliefs. God is forgiving because that is who God is, and

---

130.   Luke 7:47.

who God desires us to be as well. What prevents us from becoming forgiving and merciful is the religious idea of righteousness. Righteousness is what prevents us from hearing Jesus' words, just as righteousness prevented the religious people of Jesus' day from hearing his words. Jesus repeatedly says that he did not come for the righteous but for sinners.

> When the Pharisees saw this, they said to his disciples, "Why does your teacher eat with tax collectors and sinners?" But when he heard this, he said, "Those who are well have no need of a physician, but those who are sick. Go and learn what this means, 'I desire mercy, not sacrifice.' For I have come to call not the righteous but sinners."[131]

Righteous people will always ignore Jesus' words, which constantly reveal our sin at ever deeper levels. Righteous people are people who are confident that they have gone far enough on the spiritual journey, but that confidence can only be maintained by ignoring the words of Jesus, which constantly tell us that our sin and need for forgiveness and mercy is greater than we imagine. Religious people tend to want enough forgiveness and mercy to cover their own sins, but not so much forgiveness and mercy that they would become God's forgiveness and mercy to the world. That is reserved for people who take Jesus' words seriously and want to become his disciples. As we have seen, however, that is usually not where we begin the spiritual journey. We usually begin by wanting salvation by having our sins forgiven. Jesus, however, never tells us how to get our sins forgiven but only how to become forgiving.

---

131.   Matthew 9:11-13; Mark 2:17; Luke 5:32.

For this reason the kingdom of heaven may be compared to a king who wished to settle accounts with his slaves. When he began the reckoning, one who owed him ten thousand talents was brought to him; and, as he could not pay, his lord ordered him to be sold, together with his wife and children and all his possessions, and payment to be made. So the slave fell on his knees before him, saying, 'Have patience with me, and I will pay you everything.' And out of pity for him, the lord of that slave released him and forgave him the debt. But that same slave, as he went out, came upon one of his fellow slaves who owed him a hundred denarii; and seizing him by the throat, he said, 'Pay what you owe.' Then his fellow slave fell down and pleaded with him, 'Have patience with me, and I will pay you.' But he refused; then he went and threw him into prison until he would pay the debt. When his fellow slaves saw what had happened, they were greatly distressed, and they went and reported to their lord all that had taken place. Then his lord summoned him and said to him, 'You wicked slave! I forgave you all that debt because you pleaded with me. Should you not have had mercy on your fellow slave, as I had mercy on you?' And in anger his lord handed him over to be tortured until he would pay his entire debt. So my heavenly Father will also do to every one of you, if you do not forgive your brother or sister from your heart."[132]

Wanting to be forgiven is different than wanting to become forgiving. The popular gospel of Christianity Lite is about how to be forgiven, but Jesus' words are about our becoming forgiving. That requires that deeper level of being in God, rather than

---

132.   Matthew 18:23-35.

being in the world. When addressing his disciple, Jesus is always speaking to who they are in God rather than who they are in the world. In order to hear his words, we need that deeper level of consciousness that gets us beneath the understanding that the world has given us. As we have seen, our inherited understanding that we receive from the world is about our surviving and prospering in the world. The man in the parable above acts out of what he knows to be his own self-interest in the world, which is to receive forgiveness but not extend it to others. In the case of the parable, wealth is the illusion that the man in the parable believes will add substance to his life. From the subject/object perspective of who we are in the world, it is good to have our debts forgiven, but it is not good from that perspective to forgive the debts of others and therein decrease our wealth. In order to forgive the debt of others we need that unitive level of consciousness that is able to see ourselves in that neighbor.

The words of Jesus are all about freedom from the world and the mind the world has given us in order that we might take on the mind of Jesus which best prepares us for eternal life. As long as we remain attached to the world and identify with that person we are in the world, we will be attracted to religions that stop with the forgiveness of sins, and avoid the words of Jesus that tell us, "If you do not forgive others, neither will your Father forgive your trespasses."[133] Forgiveness is not something that allows us to escape God's wrath but what makes us into God's forgiving likeness if we experience enough of it. Of course, we can only experience God's forgiveness through repentance or changing our minds

---

133.   Matthew 6:15, also see Mark 11:26.

about the depth of our sin, which keeps us from the fullness of life in God. God cannot forgive us unless we see our ever deeper need for forgiveness.

The reason that becoming forgiving is so important is because unforgiveness is what connects us to the world and all the wounds the world has inflicted upon us. We are connected to the world and its illusions of happiness by the wounds inflicted upon us beginning in childhood. As children, we were defenseless against such wounds, but our growing exposure to the world revealed that some people seemed to be above being wounded because their wealth, power, or fame allowed them to defend themselves against such wounds. Much of our life in the world is directed by the unconscious desire to avoid the painful wounds of childhood. If we lack access to wealth, power, or prestige, we might choose humor, anger, or a host of other devises to deal with the original sins that were done to us and which have molded our lives in the world, often beneath our notice. On the unconscious level, and sometimes even on the conscious level, we try to deal with those wounds by never letting them happen again. Jesus' solution is quite different. What removes those wounds, or those sins that had been done to us and have been directing our lives on both a conscious and unconscious level, is forgiveness. The forgiveness of sins is what sets us free. Jesus says, "If you forgive the sins of any, they are forgiven them; if you retain the sins of any, they are retained."[134] Our forgiveness of the sins that were done to us not only set those who wounded us free but it sets us free from those wounds as well. What retains the wounds is our

134.   John 20:23.

unforgiveness and our desire to see those sinners punished. Our forgiveness of others is what sets us free from the world and the hold the world has upon us. We have the power to heal ourselves through our forgiveness of others, but that is very contrary to the way the world has taught us to be. In the world, our instinct is to respond in kind, but when we are *in* God, we respond to evil with forgiveness, which defeats evil and stops it from infecting us. According to Jesus, our wounds are only healed through our forgiveness of those who have wounded us. We want to believe that we have received God's forgiveness, but the wounds remain until we become God's forgiveness to those who have wounded us. Jesus from the Cross prays for his torturers to be forgiven,[135] in order that he would be free from the wounds they inflicted upon him. Unforgiveness is what keeps us enslaved to the sins that were done to us.

The world tells us that we are only liable for the sins that we commit, but Jesus tells us that we are more liable for the sins that were done to us. Christianity Lite focus on getting God to forgive our sins, but Jesus' words focus on getting us to forgive the sins that were done to us. The sins that were committed against us are what keep us connected to the world, and the ways of the world. God's forgiveness is freely given, but our forgiveness of others is what releases us from the hold that the world has upon us. Forgiveness is not something to merely receive through a belief, but something to become in order to be set free.

Christianity Lite thinks it's about getting our personal sins forgiven by God, but Jesus is always calling us to forgive in order

---

135.   Luke 23:34.

to be set free from the sins of others, which often direct our lives beneath our notice. Forgiveness is not something we do simply for other people. It is more importantly something we do for ourselves in order to be free. Likewise, God does not forgive us because of something we do, but because of who God is. If we are still making decisions about who we should forgive, who we should show mercy toward, and who we should love, the world still has a hold of us and we have not gone very far on the spiritual journey to which Jesus calls us. Forgiveness, mercy, and love are what free us to be *in* God rather than *in* the world.

There are no conditions to God's forgiveness and love, and there should be no conditions to our forgiveness and love. In order to be God's forgiveness to the world, we have to become forgiving and not merely forgiven. That is the message Jesus is trying to convey with the above statement that if you do not forgive others, God cannot complete the forgiveness in us. Being forgiven only gets us half way there. Becoming God's forgiveness to the world is what completes God's ultimate desire for us and sets us free from the world in order to realize our deeper life in God.

If we are still identifying with the person we are in the world, there are always conditions for our forgiveness of others. From our perspective in the world, we imagine that God must have conditions for his forgiveness and love as well. From our perspective in the world, we want to know what God's conditions are for forgiving us. Jesus, however, never tells us how to get our sins forgiven, but instead tells us to forgive everyone in order to be free from the hold the world has upon us. "For freedom Christ has set us free."[136] Early on in the spiritual, we can only imagine that as a freedom from sin. If we spend time alone with God and Jesus' words, however, we come to experience that deeper freedom from unforgiveness, which releases the hold the world has upon us.

God has given us the enormous freedom to create the nature of the eternal being. What determines our eternal nature is how much, or how little, of Jesus' words has taken root at the core of our being. The things we love and pursue in life are what shape who we are, and who we eventually become. God does not judge us according to the beliefs we profess or the tribes to which we belong. God does not judge us at all but allows us to create our own eternal being by the things we choose to love. God loves forgiveness, mercy, and love because God is free and desires his daughters and sons to be free as well, but our freedom also allows us to choose the things we love. Jesus tells us the best things to love in order that we might be like his our heavenly Father. God is not interested in the epistemic truths that human beings create with their doctrines and theories. God is interested in our being, and Jesus tells us the best way to be by telling us the best things to love.

From the perspective of who we are in the world, there appear to be good people and bad people, but, as we have seen, the person we are in the world is largely the result of wounds we received in childhood, and our largely unconscious response to those wounds. Those wounds that the world inflicts upon us produce people who the world sees as either good or bad according to the world's values. If we identify with who we are in the world

---

136.   Galatians 5:1.

because our wounds have produced good people by the world's standards, we will never hear Jesus' words calling us to repent for being who we are in the world. If we believe that God judges us based upon what the world considers our sins, we are not paying attention to Jesus' words. God does not judge us according to what the world considers our sins. In fact, God does not judge us at all but rather allows us to create the nature of our eternal being by the things we choose to love. The things that Jesus tells us to love are never the things the world tells us to love. As long as we identify with the world, and who we are in the world, rather than who we are in God at the core of our being, we will live according to the world's ways rather than the deeper life to which Jesus calls us.

> When Jesus had finished speaking, a Pharisee invited him to eat with him; so he went in and reclined at the table. But the Pharisee was surprised when he noticed that Jesus did not first wash before the meal. Then the Lord said to him, "Now then, you Pharisees clean the outside of the cup and dish, but inside you are full of greed and wickedness. You foolish people! Did not the one who made the outside make the inside also? But now as for what is inside you—be generous to the poor, and everything will be clean for you.[137]

Religious people are always worried about sin and being unclean because of their sin, which they believe puts them at odds with God, but Jesus is always speaking about the divine virtues that cover a multitude of sins. Of course, when God is seen from the subject/object perspective as a distant sovereign who demand

---

137. Luke 11:37-41. NIV

obedience and punishes disobedience, the forgiveness of our sins is paramount, but when God is experienced as a loving Father, the divine virtues of which Jesus speaks becomes our chief concern because we desire to love what God loves. Many forms of the Christian religion teach the forgiveness of sins, but Jesus' disciples know that Jesus is not teaching us how to get our sins forgiven, but how to develop the heavenly virtues of which Jesus' speaks. "Above all, maintain constant love for one another, for love covers a multitude of sins."[138]

Christianity Lite tells us how to get our sins forgiven; Jesus tells us that our sin is deeper than we imagine but so is God's forgiveness and mercy. The popular forms of Christianity equate being forgiven with righteousness; Jesus tells us that the purpose of God's forgiveness and mercy is to make us forgiving and merciful. What is so attractive about Christianity Lite is that if God has conditions for forgiving us, we can have conditions for forgiveness as well, but those conditions are what keep us connected to the world and the hold it has upon us.

From our left-brain's perspective of being in the world, survival shapes our being and always places our interests above the interests of others. If we live exclusively out of the left-brain's understanding that the world has given us, we will always insist that we must first love ourselves before we can love others, and forgiveness will always be conditional. On occasion, however, we may experience that other level of consciousness that is able to see our neighbor, and sometimes even our enemy, as more important than ourselves. This is the level of consciousness to which Jesus

---

138.   1 Peter 4:8.

is always calling us. It is the moral level of consciousness where
we are able to see another person's needs as greater than our own,
because we possess an alternative level of unitive consciousness
that sees no distinction between ourselves and our neighbor. How
much we exercise that alternative level of consciousness is what
determines how far we go in the spiritual journey. Some, who
never experience that alternative level of unitive consciousness
because their lives are exclusively in the world, may act morally
at times for fear of being thought to only care about themselves,
but it is merely an act. In order to actually love our neighbor as
ourselves requires that alternative level of unitive consciousness
that sees our neighbor as part of that larger Being that we all are
in God. Immanuel Kant (1724-1804) referred to it as the categor-
ical imperative, or that part of our mind that allows us to reason
morally and not merely in our own self-interest. Kant argued that
in order to be moral beings we should only do what we would
want everyone else to do in same situation. The way Jesus puts it
is, "In everything do to others as you would have them do to you;
for this is the law and the prophets."[139] This requires that unitive
level of consciousness that sees oneself in God in the same way
that everyone else is in God, rather than seeing God and other
human beings as objects different from ourselves. How much or
how little we choose to operate out of that unitive consciousness
is what ultimately determines how much of Jesus' words we will
be willing to make our own.

Faith has very little to do with the religious doctrines we profess to believe, except for the fact that that is where we usually
begin the spiritual journey. Faith is much more about how deeply

---

139.   Matthew 7:12.

we are willing to go into this other level of unitive consciousness that allows us to see the beauty and goodness of Jesus' words. As we have said, the great spiritual question is how far do we want to go with Jesus? How far do we want to go with the forgiveness that Jesus reveals from the cross? We all want our sins forgiven, but do we want the sins of the entire world forgiven, including the sins of our enemies? Do we want their sins forgiven because we have become so aware of our sins being forgiven at ever greater depths that we have been transformed into forgiving creatures? Jesus' words are always about increasing our need for forgiveness in order that we might become ever more forgiving.

Many people love the Bible because, from our subject/object perspective in the world, it gives us a basis from which to judge the righteous from sinners. Likewise, we hate the words of Jesus that tell us not to judge because we judge by human standards and Jesus judges no one. "You judge by human standards; I judge no one."[140] Mercy is the virtue of not judging. It is the absence of judgment, and the more mercy we are aware of receiving, the more merciful we become. "Go and learn what this means, 'I desire mercy, not sacrifice.' For I have come to call not the righteous but sinners."[141] Only sinners can be Jesus' disciples, because in order to be his forgiveness and mercy to the world, we have to become the recipients of his transformative forgiveness and mercy at ever deeper levels of our being. Indeed, we only love much because we are aware of having been forgiven much.[142]

---

140.   John 8:15
141.   Matthew 9:13; Matthew 12:7
142.   Luke 7:47.

Jesus wants to reduce us to love in order that we might be his forgiveness and mercy to the world. That requires a daily process of changing our minds in order to get ever closer to the Jesus perspective. From our perspective in the world, we want to be judged as righteous, but Jesus repeatedly says that he did not come for the righteous but only for sinners who want to be made into his likeness by being reduced to love.

Jesus tells us that God is "our Father" and wants us to be like our Father in terms of forgiveness, mercy, and love. Becoming forgiving and merciful does not happen on the epistemic level of our beliefs. On the epistemic level, we can believe that we have received forgiveness and mercy, but we only become forgiving and merciful when it becomes part of our being rather than merely a belief. That requires a different level of consciousness; specifically a level of consciousness that is able to give root to his words.

Scientists tell us that our left-brain houses most of the kind of language that is associated with the theories and maps that our cultural ethos provides, but the right-brain seems to give us access to experiences that transcend language and the kind of understanding that language provides. Unfortunately, the world, and especially the modern world of science and religion, has told us that unless our experiences can be verified by others, they are the products of the imagination and not ultimately real. Our modern minds have been taught to believe what everyone else believes, so we retreat into our cultural and religious tribes and try to find security in believing what everyone else in our little world believes. Jesus' words, however, can never be heard from that perspective. This is why Jesus tells us that we must be born

again or born from above.[143] The born again experience is a return
to our original unitive level of consciousness or who we were in
God before the world got a hold of us and wounded us with sin.
Once we begin to identity with that person we were in God before
the world got a hold of us, we not only see our own innocence,
but even the innocence of our enemies. This is the perspective that
allows Jesus from the Cross to ask his Father to forgive his torturers, "for they do not know what they are doing."[144]

In order for us to get to that place from which we can forgive
as Jesus forgives, we not only need to be born again, or get back
to who we were in God before the world got a hold of us, but we
also have to end the life we have created for ourselves in order to
be in the world. The person we are in the world has to die in order
for our new life in God to come forth.

> Very truly, I tell you, unless a grain of wheat falls into the
> earth and dies, it remains just a single grain; but if it dies it
> bears much fruit. Those who love their life lose it, and those
> who hate their life in this world will keep it for eternal life.[145]

The single grain is who we are in the world of the subject/
object perspective. That self, and its perspective, has to die in
order to realize who we are in God from the perspective of our
original unitive consciousness that unites us with God and all
other human beings. When we begin to identify with who we were
in God before the world got a hold of us, we begin to see that Jesus
not only takes away our sin, but our guilt and the guilt of others as

---

143.   John 3:3.
144.   Luke 23:34.
145.   John 12:24-25.

well. We are all products of the sins inflicted upon us in childhood, which made us into the people we eventually become. As we have said, some of those wounds made us into horrible sinners and others into the kind of righteous people with whom Jesus always had trouble. Jesus always prefers sinners to righteous people, since it seems easier for them to accept the death of the false-self in order to discover who they were in God before the world got a hold of them. Jesus came to redeem the world from sin. He shows us how that is done through forgiveness, but the religious response of our false-self is, "No, you do it Jesus, and we will participate in your forgiveness of sin through our belief rather than our becoming your forgiveness and mercy to the world."

As we have said, Jesus offers his forgiveness and mercy to everyone, but not as something to receive as a belief but rather as something to become. It is not the epistemic belief that we have been forgiven, but the ontological reality that we have become forgiving as our heavenly Father is forgiving. Recall Jesus saying that, "if you do not forgive others, neither will your Father forgive your trespasses."[146] Forgiveness has to be real and not a mere belief. We can only forgive everyone when we are able to see a God that forgives everyone. Until we get to that place in the spiritual journey, we can only see a God that forgives people like us that have the right religious beliefs. These were the only people Jesus had trouble with in his day and things have not changed.

Faith is not an epistemic belief in the right religious doctrines, but a way of being that draws us ever deeper into the life to which Jesus calls us. The life to which Jesus calls us is not about

---

146.   Matthew 6:15, also see Mark 11:26.

adding substance to our lives but about reducing us to forgiveness, mercy, and love. That reduction is the consequence of a lifetime practice of prayer, whereby the ongoing experience of God's presence and Jesus' words cause the things of the world to grow dim and no longer have the hold upon us they once had.

Hearing the words of Jesus requires an innocence and openness of mind, which is very different from the closed mindedness and quasi certainty of the religious doctrines that we house in our left-brain's understanding of the world. Hearing Jesus' words is an apophatic experience, while our religious doctrines are part of the understanding we have inherited from the world; and our inherited understanding of world is the very thing that prevents us from hearing the words of Jesus. Indeed, Jesus' words are never compatible with the understanding we inherit from the world, and that almost always includes our religious understanding as well. It is only the raw experience of Jesus' words that transforms us, but that experience requires a different level of consciousness than that level of consciousness through which we generally deal with the world. It is the level of consciousness that is able to experience the apophatic and ineffable, rather than that level of consciousness that purports to know and understand. Most religions are made for people in the world. Jesus' disciples are people who are committed to his kingdom and bringing it to earth because their identity is not in the world. Religions tell us what to believe, Jesus tells us how to be.

There is a problem, however, with seeing the gospel as a matter of becoming God's forgiveness, mercy, and love to the world rather than being the recipients of such things through our religious beliefs. The problem with building our lives upon the divine virtues of which Jesus speaks is that it is often accused of being a works gospel and something that we do instead of something that God does. That should be a genuine concern, but building our lives upon Jesus' words is not something we do but something that God does by bringing about the death of the false-self. If we try to develop these virtues on our own, they are just the product of the false-self, and intended to make ourselves appear forgiving, merciful, and loving to the world. It is not through effort but through our death that we become the creatures that God desires us to be. Our part in becoming Jesus' disciples is simply to give God permission to work through the circumstances of our lives to bring about the death of the false-self, in order that our true self, or who we are in God, might come forth.

CHAPTER EIGHT

The Death of the False-Self

Jesus did not preach religious doctrines. He preached the death of the false-self, which holds both our shame and our righteousness. Only with the death of the false-self are we reduced to who we are in God, and only who we are in God can give root to the heavenly virtues to which Jesus' words call us. The false-self is the self that is different from other selves because it is either better or worse than others based upon a great variety of criterion the world has given us. A God that is "our Father", however, loves all of his daughters and sons with the same love and calls us to love all of God's children as our sisters and brothers. Religion, however, is almost always tribal with a god that only loves those sisters and brothers that behave and believe as we do. That is not a Father/ God who loves and wants to redeem all of his daughters and sons into the fullness of eternal life in God. Of course, God has made us free and we get to choose how much of that fullness of life we want, but that choice is a matter of how much death we are willing to suffer in order for the reign of God to come forth in our lives. I remember seeing a great bumper sticker several years ago that said, "The only good Christian is a dead Christian." Who we are in the world has to die in order that who we are in God might come forth.

The Bible is God's revelation of his relationship with human beings, and as such it largely reflects who human beings believe God to be. Jesus, on the other hand, is the word of God or the most that can be revealed about an infinite and eternal God that is always beyond our understanding but not our experience. What Jesus' words reveal is not who God is, but who we should be as God's daughters and sons. Jesus is not simply the incarnation of the Divine but the incarnation of God's son. Thus, Jesus' words tell us how to be as God's daughters and sons. From that, however, we can deduce the nature of "our Father" because a loving father desires his children to be as he is in character and virtue. We know that "our Father" must forgive everyone and judge no one because Jesus tells us to forgive everyone[147] and judge no one.[148]

As we have said, the most important thing to know about God is that he is "our Father" and from that we can deduce that Jesus' words are telling us how to be in order that we would be like our heavenly Father. As we have seen, knowing God as our Father is very different from knowing God as a distant sovereign who desires obedience and punishes disobedience. Recall the story of the Prodigal where the older brother wants his obedience rewarded but does not want to become forgiving and merciful like his father.

The ultimate question at the base of the spiritual journey to which Jesus calls us is how much do you want to resemble our heavenly Father rather than the world? That cannot be answered with a belief. Our beliefs are part of the false-self that we and the

147.   Matthew 6:15.
148.   Matthew 7:1-2.

world have created in order to be in the world. What determines the nature of our eternal being are our loves. Do we love the things that the world tells us to love or the things Jesus tells us to love?

We love the false-self because it is at least partially our own creation. The more we see it as our own creation, the more we love it and the less we want to see it die in order for our life in God to come forth. This is why it is not a blessing to be rich, powerful, or famous, and one of the reasons why Jesus says he came "to bring good news to the poor."[149] We only come into our deeper life in God through the death of the false-self. That is the deep repentance that Jesus is always calling us to in order to be his disciples. It is repentance or changing our minds about who we are and therein seeing our sin at ever deeper levels. That is the nature of the spiritual journey. The ultimate sin that stops the spiritual journey into Jesus' forgiving and merciful likeness is our claim to righteousness. In all three of the synoptic Gospels, Jesus says, that he has "come to call not the righteous but sinners to repentance."[150] Only the sinner is open to the transformative power of God's forgiveness and mercy. Jesus' words are constantly calling us to see our sin at ever deeper levels. What prevents us from hearing those words is the pretense of the false-self to righteousness.

> Two men went up to the temple to pray, one a Pharisee and the other a tax collector. The Pharisee, standing by himself, was praying thus, 'God, I thank you that I am not like other people: thieves, rogues, adulterers, or even like this tax collector. I fast twice a week; I give a tenth of all my income.' But

---

149. Luke 4:18.
150. Luke 5:32, Matthew 9:11-13, and Mark 2:17.

the tax collector, standing far off, would not even look up to heaven, but was beating his breast and saying, 'God, be merciful to me, a sinner!' I tell you, this man went down to his home justified rather than the other; for all who exalt themselves will be humbled, but all who humble themselves will be exalted.[151]

Shakespeare was right, "All the world's a stage, and all the men and women merely players;"[152] but there is the deeper life of which Jesus speaks. Of course, if we like the play and the role we have been given in the play, we have little interest in a deeper life. The most blessed among us are those who have experienced the kind of tragedies in their life that destroy the illusions of the false-self, and especially the false-self's claim to righteousness. Jesus' words reveal our sin and need for forgiveness and mercy at ever deeper levels. Righteousness is what prevents us from hearing those words.

We can only minister forgiveness and mercy by being the constant recipients of forgiveness and mercy. The false-self's pretense to righteousness through its beliefs and behavior is what stops the flow of God's forgiveness and mercy to the world. The righteousness of the false-self is what allows us to judge the sins of others, just as it was the sin of the religious leaders of Jesus' day. This is why Jesus tells us not to judge, since judgment is always rooted in righteousness, and being righteous is always what stops the transformative flow of God's forgiveness and mercy. God's forgiveness and mercy is not intended to make the false-self appear

---

151.   Luke 18:10-14.
152.   Shakespeare. *As You Like It.* Act II, Scene VII.

righteous. God's forgiveness and mercy is intended to equip us to be God's forgiveness and mercy to the world. In order for that to happen, we have to see our sin and need for repentance at ever deeper levels until there is nothing left of the false-self's identity and claim to righteousness. That is not always immediately apparent, however, and it may take years before we realize that God's forgiveness and mercy are intended to equip the true self or who we are in God, rather than to make the false-self appear righteous. This is why Jesus tells us not to judge, since judgment is always based in righteousness.

> Do not judge, so that you may not be judged. For with the judgment you make you will be judged, and the measure you give will be the measure you get. Why do you see the speck in your neighbor's eye, but do not notice the log in your own eye? Or how can you say to your neighbor, 'Let me take the speck out of your eye,' while the log is in your own eye? You hypocrite, first take the log out of your own eye, and then you will see clearly to take the speck out of your neighbor's eye.[153]

The common interpretation of this passage is that the log in our own eye is some sin, and that sin has to be removed before we can remove the sin in someone else's eye. Thus, the interpretation is that we have to be sinless in order to deal with another person's sin. The deeper interpretation, which is more consistent with Jesus' teachings, is that the sin which has to be removed from our own eye is the sin of righteousness. God is good at forgiving sins and wants us to be good at it as well. The way we become

---

153.   Matthew 7:1-5.

good at forgiveness and mercy is by receiving it at ever deeper levels. What prevents us from receiving forgiveness and mercy at ever deeper levels is the idea of righteousness as the result of our religious beliefs. We only become forgiving and merciful by being the constant recipients of God's forgiveness and mercy because we pay attention to Jesus' words and the repentance to which they constantly call us.

The idea that we have been made righteous through our religious beliefs is what ends the spiritual journey into those deeper levels of being *in God* to which Jesus is always calling us. People who believe they are righteous because of their religious beliefs are what Jesus refers to as hypocrites. Hypocrites are people who profess beliefs that are contrary to the reality of their lives. Believing that your religious beliefs have made you righteous, in spite of your behavior to the contrary, is what hypocrisy is. A Christian hypocrite is someone who claims to be a follower of Jesus but pay no attention to the words of Jesus and the life to which those words call us. A hypocrite is someone who professes beliefs, but they are just the beliefs of the false-self or who we want other people, ourselves, and God to believe we are. A hypocrite is someone who wants other people to believe they are righteous, but their righteousness is just a belief about them being sinless due to their beliefs, rather than their being transformed into Jesus' forgiving and merciful likeness.

When Jesus says, "take the log out of your own eye, and then you will see clearly to take the speck out of your neighbor's eye" he is speaking about two different things: a log and a speck. The speck is sin, which God has little trouble dealing with, but the log is righteousness which puts us beyond the transformative power of God's forgiveness. Only people who are actively experiencing God's forgiveness and mercy flowing through their own repentance can minister forgiveness and mercy to others. Only sinners can minister to sinners. That is the great wisdom behind Alcoholics Anonymous, which Christianity Lite never seems to get. Jesus says that he only came for sinners and not the righteous, because those who believe they are righteous through their beliefs and religious practices have decided that they have gone far enough with God and are no longer in need of forgiveness and mercy. In order to maintain that righteousness, however, they have to avoid the words of Jesus or trust that their religious beliefs trump the words of Jesus, which are always calling us to deeper levels of repentance and transformation.

Sin, at its deepest level, is our lack of forgiveness, mercy, and love toward others. The recognition of that deep sin and our repentance or changing our minds about our own need for forgiveness and mercy is what allows us to become God's conduits of forgiveness and mercy to the world. Evangelizing the world through a sense of righteousness because of what we believe is the kind of evangelism that Jesus condemns.

> But woe to you, scribes and Pharisees, hypocrites! For you
> cross seas and land to make a single convert, and you make
> the new convert twice as much a child of hell as yourself.[154]

Ministering forgiveness and mercy can never be done from a place of righteousness. The righteousness to which Jesus calls us is about becoming ever more like our heavenly Father in terms of

---

154.   Matthew 23:15.

forgiveness, mercy, and love, because Jesus' words have revealed our own need of forgiveness and mercy at ever deeper levels. As we have seen, being the agents of God's forgiveness and mercy is very different from being the recipients of God's forgiveness and mercy.

The false-self, however, has to be content with righteousness as the forgiveness of sins, since the false-self cannot hear the words of Jesus and the deep repentance to which they call us for being who we are in the world rather than being who we are in God. Jesus always had problems with religious people, since religion in its more popular forms is usually little more than a masquerade party for the false-self. Offering salvation for the false-self is what popular religions offer, Jesus never does. He says,

> If any want to become my followers, let them deny themselves and take up their cross and follow me. For those who want to save their life will lose it, and those who lose their life for my sake will find it. For what will it profit them if they gain the whole world but forfeit their life?[155]

Jesus is always speaking about our eternal life and not our life in the world. This is also why his words cannot be heard or taken seriously from the perspective of who we are in the world. The false-self has to die in order for the reign of God to come forth in our life, but the death of the false-self is not something that we can bring about on our own. It is rather something that happens behind our backs, if we spend enough time in God's presence and Jesus' words that we begin to identify with who we are in God

---

155.   Matthew 16:24-26.

rather than the person we are in the world. If we seldom go to that deep place of prayer, Christianity Lite is as far as we can go in the spiritual journey, since the false-self, or who we are in the world, is only capable of hearing what is compatible with our life in the world.

Of course, we all begin the spiritual journey with the false-self, or the cultural self to use Richard Niebuhr's (1894-1962) language, but there is the deeper self of who we were in God before the world got a hold of us and began making us into its likeness. As we have seen, our perspective from that deeper self that we are in God is very different from the perspective the world has given us. Only when the false-self is out of the way can we hear the words of Jesus:

> But I say to you that listen, Love your enemies, do good to those who hate you, bless those who curse you, pray for those who abuse you. If anyone strikes you on the cheek, offer the other also; and from anyone who takes away your coat do not withhold even your shirt. Give to everyone who begs from you; and if anyone takes away your goods, do not ask for them again.[156]

From our perspective in the world, Jesus' words are nonsense, so we quite literally do not listen, but Jesus says, "To you that *listen*, Love your enemies and do good to those who hate you." Jesus is telling us about his kingdom and the virtues that establish our identity in his kingdom. God offers eternal life to everyone but we get to choose the nature of that eternal life by the

---

156.   Luke 6:27-30.

things we choose to love in this life. We are made in God image with love at the core of our being, but God has also made us free, and out of that freedom we create our own eternal nature by the things we attach our love to in this life. The things that the world tells us to love are very different from the things that Jesus tells us to love.

The popular gospel tells us how to get our sins forgiven through our beliefs, and once we have been forgiven, the popular gospel tells us we are fit for heaven just as we are. Jesus tells a very different story about becoming his disciples by allowing his words to take root at the core of our being in order that we might become like him and fit for his heavenly kingdom.

> Enter through the narrow gate; for the gate is wide and the road is easy that leads to destruction, and there are many who take it. For the gate is narrow and the road is hard that leads to life, and there are few who find it.[157]

Who we are in the world has too much baggage to pass through the narrow gate. Only who we are in God is little enough to pass through and unencumbered enough to endure the hard road. To proceed on the journey into the fullness of life, we have to shed all of those possessions or things that possess the false-self and give it its meaning and distinguish it from other false-selves. Only who we are in God is able to love our enemies and bless those who curse us because we are no longer identified by our enemies and those that curse us. We are being transformed by a lifetime of repentance in response to Jesus' words, until we have

---

157.   Matthew 7:13-14.

experienced so much mercy and forgiveness that there is nothing left of the false-self that previously held all of our judgments and unforgiveness. Repentance and the experience of God's forgiveness and mercy at ever deeper levels is what reduce us to love.

It is the world that has taught the false-self who and what to love, and who and what to hate, but Jesus' words seek to free us from that false-self in order that we might freely love as God loves without restriction. Of course, as long as we identify with our own false-self, we will imagine that God is like us and loves what we love and hates what we hate. The god of the false-self is the god of this world who tells us who our enemies are and who we should love and not love. It is the world that teaches us how to gain advantage over others in order to achieve happiness, at the cost of others. As long as we identify with that false-self that the world has persuaded us to be, we will always find ways around the words of Jesus, which is easy enough because the false-self can never really hear the nonsensical words of Jesus. In order to hear Jesus' words and take them seriously, we need to identify with that deeper level of consciousness that allows us to experience our being in God rather than our being in the world. Only that deeper self of who we were in God before the world got a hold of us is capable of giving root to Jesus' words. Thus, the more time we spend in prayer identifying with who we are in God, the less hold the world has upon us. The false-self dies from attrition or weakening because the things that the world tells us to love no longer possess us and we no longer give our attention to them. This is the dying before we die in order to see the beauty of the gospel as a way to be, rather than merely a belief that promises a way to avoid God's judgment.

Jesus, however, tells us that God does not judge us at all. "The Father judges no one but has given all judgment to the Son."[158] Likewise, Jesus tells us that he judges no one. "You judge by human standards; I judge no one."[159] Indeed, Jesus tells us that we will be allowed to judge ourselves by the way we judge others. "For with the judgment you make you will be judged, and the measure you give will be the measure you get."[160] It is the world that has taught us to judge, but Jesus' words constantly call us to repent or change our minds concerning our judgment of others. The world teaches us how to distinguish between the righteous and sinners, but Jesus tells us that very judgment is the sin of the false-self, which imagines it can know the heart of God and God's relationship with another human being. We are not called to judge the sins of others but only to be God's forgiveness, mercy, and love to the world. How far we go on this spiritual journey into the deeper life to which Jesus calls us is a matter of how much death we are willing to bear. This is the deeper meaning of the cross and Jesus' words: "pick up your cross and follow me."[161]

Life begins after death, but we get to choose when we die. Some wait until their heart stops beating and they take their last breath; others decide to die early and allow the false-self, which we and the world have created, to die in order that our life in God may begin as soon as possible. This is the reign of God that we are able to participate in if we allow the false-self to die, and we come to identify with who we are in God rather than who we are in the world.

---

158.   John 5:22.
159.   John 8:15.
160.   Matthew 7:2.
161.   Matthew 10:38, 16:24; Mark 8:34; Luke 9:23, 14:27.

Of course, the false-self cannot die until we are aware of the deeper life we have in God and prefer that deeper life to our life in the world. Prayer is that different level of consciousness through which we access that deeper life. Prayer, at its deepest level, is awareness in its purest form. In our normal state of consciousness, awareness is what we use to focus upon the things the world tells us to focus upon, but in prayer, our awareness is turned in on itself. It is the opening of our mind to what is beyond what we know. The world has taught us what we need to know, but that knowledge is the very thing that keeps us from hearing the words of Jesus. What opens us to hearing his words is that pure consciousness or awareness that refuses to focus on any of the things that the world tells us to fix our attention upon. The practice of pure awareness is the silence and stillness that gives us access to Jesus' words. It is that level of consciousness that is deeper than all of the knowing with which the world has equipped us.

At the deepest level of our being, we are consciousness itself, and how we direct that consciousness is determined by what we love, and what we love ultimately determines the nature of our eternal being. Jesus' words tell us the best things to love and the worst things to love. God has given human beings the enormous freedom to create their own eternal nature by the things they choose to love. Jesus is trying to teach us how to direct that love in order that we might enjoy the fullness of eternal life. This is what Jesus' disciples understand. The Gospels are about love and how to direct our love in order that we might be as God desires us to be, but we are also free and able to direct that love as we wish in order to become the eternal creature we choose to be.

The early twentieth century Spanish philosopher Jose Ortega y Gasset (1883-1955) claimed that love was most essentially a matter of attention abnormally fixed. In life, our attention is all over the place, until we fall in love, and then that person or that thing toward which we direct our love and attention begins to mold our very being. This attention, or love, attaches us to things just the way fear can attach us to things. If we identify with who we are in the world, we will come to love and fear the things the world tells us to love and fear. If we spend enough time in that apophatic experience of prayer that gives us access to Jesus' words, we will come to love and fear those things that Jesus tells us to love and fear.

> Do not store up for yourself treasures on earth, where moth and rust consume and where thieves break in and steal; but store up for yourselves treasures in heaven, where neither moth nor rust consumes and where thieves do not break in and steal. For where your treasure is, there your heart will be also.[162]

The belief that our being can be shaped by our beliefs rather than our love is the great lie especially true of our modern age.

> Not everyone who says to me, 'Lord, Lord,' will enter the kingdom of heaven, but only the one who does the will of my Father in heaven. On that day many will say to me, 'Lord, Lord, did we not prophesy in your name, and cast out demons in your name, and do many deeds of power in your

---

162.   Matthew 6:19-21.

name?' Then I will declare to them, 'I never knew you; go away from me, you evildoers.'[163]

Everyone loves the name of Jesus, but his words are another matter. We can easily profess to love Jesus, but if we do not give our attention to his words and the kind of prayerful perspective that can make sense of his words, we have the kind of religion that Jesus warns us against. The gospel is not some religious doctrine to believe, but the deeper life to which Jesus' words call us. How far into that deeper life we go is what determines the nature of our eternal being. Jesus tells us to abide in his love, and we do that by keeping his commandments. "If you keep my commandments, you will abide in my love, just as I have kept my Father's commandments and abide in his love."[164]

> I have said these things to you so that my joy may be in you,
> and that your joy may be complete. This is my command-
> ment, that you love one another as I have loved you.[165]

Loving one another, as Jesus has loved us, is impossible from our perspective in the world. In the world, the subject/object perspective of the left-brain is always reading things from the perspective of an individual subject surrounded by a world of objects. This left-brain perspective is essential to our survival in the world, but from that perspective, we can never love our enemy, or even our neighbor as ourselves. Loving others the way Jesus loves us requires a radically different level of consciousness, which is

---

163.   Matthew 7:21-23.
164.   John 15:10.
165.   John 15:11.

not concerned with our own survival because we are safe and in another Being. Jesus knew he was in the Father, and the Father was in him. Being in God is that original, unitive consciousness of being secure in another being where we no longer need to be concerned with our own needs, but can focus our attention on loving something other than ourselves. That is the radically different level of consciousness to which Jesus is calling us. When Jesus tells us, "Repent, for the kingdom of heaven has come near"[166], he is not telling us to be remorseful over our sins in order to have our sins forgiven, although that is what we will hear from our subject/object perspective in the world. The repentance to which Jesus calls us is the much deeper repentance of changing our minds about who we are.

The popular gospel tells us how to get the sins of the false-self forgiven, but Jesus' gospel tells us how to be the person that God created rather than the person the world created. In making us free, God allows us to direct our love and thus create our own eternal being as we wish. God will love us no matter what we choose, but we will spend eternity with beings that love what we love, so choose wisely.

We have bicameral brains because we are both in the world and in God. When Jesus speaks to his disciples, he is speaking to who they are in God. Of course, sometimes Jesus is speaking to who we are in the world. That is certainly the case when he speaks to the religious leaders of his day. They are unaware of any deeper life in God, and believe that they can make the false-self presentable to God by what they believe and how they act, rather than by

---

166.   Matthew 4:17.

what they love. Christianity Lite preaches salvation for the false-self through our beliefs; Jesus preached the death of the false-self in order that the reign of God might come forth in that deeper life that we are in God.

The ultimate goal in life is to discover our true self or who we are in God, but that discovery and the life that comes out of it, only happens through the death of the false-self. Of course, early on in the spiritual journey, the false-self is usually the only self of which we are aware. It is the person that the world's standards and values have created. If that person is deemed good by the world's standards, it will be difficult for them to hear the words of Jesus, which reveal our deepest sin of wanting to be who we are in the world rather than that deeper self that we are in God. What reveals the lie of the false-self are the words of Jesus, but they can easily enough be avoided by simply never going to that deep place of prayer where we identify with who we were in God before the world got a hold of us. The only thing that can reveal the lie of the false-self is that deeper level of consciousness that puts us in touch with who we are in God at the core of our being. As we have seen, this is the level of consciousness that Jesus and the mystics understood as prayer. It is also the only level of consciousness from which we can make sense of Jesus' words.

We claim to want to know God, but knowing is the very thing that ends the spiritual journey to which Jesus calls us. The false-self is the knowing self that the world has created. Jesus' words are never compatible with the knowing the world has given us. This is why prayer, as a different level of consciousness from that level of consciousness that directs our lives in the world, is so important.

The knowing mind is the mind we inherit from the world. It is the mind that filters out the crazy things that Jesus says, but there arc deeper levels of consciousness that allow us to experience the beauty and goodness of Jesus words, but we need to practice that altered state of consciousness by identifying with who we are in God rather than the person we are in the world.

We can only hear what we are open to hear. What closes our mind is what we claim to know. The knowing mind is the mind that has been made up. Spending time in the silence of God's presence is what opens us to the beauty and goodness of Jesus' words. Prayer, as the experience of God's presence, is what allows us to see that deeper story of which Jesus speaks. Prayer, as getting away from the world and who we are in the world, is what allows us to hear Jesus' words and the deeper message of the Gospels. Our sin is not this or that particular behavior that offends God, but our life in the world which keeps us from our ultimate happiness in God. Our life and identity in the world is what causes us to respond to violence with violence,[167] and causes us not to give to all who beg from us.[168] It is only the false-self that has enemies that we cannot love. It is only the false-self that judges others based upon all the understanding the world has given us in order to direct our lives; and it is only the false-self that experiences wounds that cannot be forgiven.

Jesus' words can never take root in the false-self that we have created in order to be in the world. Prayer is that other level of consciousness where the world no longer has a hold of us, and we

---

167.   Matthew 5:39.
168.   Matthew 5:42.

can hear the words of Jesus. It is the mystic experience of being in God, rather than being in the world, and it is what allows us to see the beauty and goodness of his words. It is also what allows us to go from seeing the beauty and goodness of being forgiven, to seeing the beauty and goodness of becoming forgiving and merciful. From our perspective in the world, we cannot see why it would be advantageous for us to become forgiving or merciful. How is my suffering the offenses of others without retaliation beautiful or good? It is not, or at least it is not from the perspective of who we are in the world. As long as we remain in the world, forgiveness looks like a good thing to receive but not a good or beautiful thing to become. This is why Jesus tells us that in addition to being born from above,[169] and returning to who we were in God before the world got a hold of us and began making us into its likeness, we also need to allow the false-self to die. The death of the false-self is the only thing that emancipates us from the wounds that have created our life in the world. The more time we spend in God's presence, and away from the world, the less of a hold the world has upon us, and the more Jesus' words are able to take root in our deeper life in God. This is the dying of the false-self that we experience as a result of prayer at its deepest level. It is where we are able to identify with God enough that we can see the lie of the false-self and give God permission to bring it to an end so we might come into the fullness of life in God.

The truth that is transmitted to us in that altered state of consciousness that is prayer is not some gnostic wisdom but simply the beauty and goodness of Jesus' words. In order to be able to see

---

169.   John 3:5-7.

the beauty and goodness of his words, we have to get alone with God and away from the world. This is why Jesus tells us not to pray in public.

> And whenever you pray, do not be like the hypocrites; for they love to stand and pray in the synagogues and at the street corners, so they may be seen by others.[170]

When we pray in public, we are praying out of that persona that we are in the world, and not who we are in God. Of course, if we never get alone with God and spend enough time in the Divine presence to develop an identity in God rather than the world, the false-self is our only self. The false-self can never hear the words of Jesus. "The reason I speak to them in parables is that 'seeing they do not perceive, and hearing they do not listen, nor do they understand.'"[171] Jesus' words are not meant for the world or who we are in the world. They are only meant for his disciples. "He did not speak to them except in parables, but he explained everything in private to his disciples."[172] Jesus' words have to be explained to us in private. They are not for the world, nor can they be heard by who we are in the world. This is why he tells his disciples who want to know his words,

> When you pray, go into your inner room, close your door and pray to your Father who is in secret, and your Father who sees what is done in secret will reward you. [173]

---

170.   Matthew 6:5.
171.   Matthew 13:13.
172.   Mark 4:34.
173.   Matthew 6:6. NAS

The great reward of prayer is that it allows us to see the beauty and goodness of Jesus' words, which can only be seen from that inner room, or that deeper self, which is who we were in God before the world got a hold of us and began shaping us into its likeness. Prayer is the place his disciples go to hear his words and be transformed by them. According to Jesus, what prevents his words from taking root and producing the fullness of life within us is the false-self and its pretense to righteousness through its religious beliefs and practices. The righteousness of the false-self was the sin of the religious people in Jesus' day, and it is still the sin of religious people today.

CHAPTER NINE

Life after Death

"So therefore, none of you can become my disciple if you do not give up all your possessions."[174] This goes way beyond material possessions and addresses all those things that possess us and keep us from the fullness of life in God. Jesus' teachings are seldom literal. His words address the spiritual side of our being and not our being in the world. They are not meant to be taken literally, since someone could give up all their material possessions and still be possessed by them. Jesus' teachings do not address our behavior, which connects us to the world, but our deeper being in God. Giving up all of our possessions is a matter of giving up all those things that constitute our identity in the world, in order to come into the fullness of our identity in God. Jesus is constantly telling us that we are more than who we are in the world, and we need to be freed from that identity that the world has given us in order to realize our deeper life in God. Detachment and disidentification with who we are in the eyes of the world is what brings us to that deeper level of consciousness from which we can see the beauty, goodness, and freedom to which Jesus' words call us.

The freedom to which Jesus calls us speaks to both the slave and the Emperor. Both are caught in illusions from which Jesus

---

174.   Luke 14:33.

wishes to free us. Of course, the slave is in the privileged position from which it is easier to see the illusion of their identity in the world, and the death of their false-self is less painful than that of the Emperor. The poor are not as attached to their identity in the world as are the rich, powerful, and famous. This is why Jesus calls the poor "blessed." In fact, Jesus gives us a perfect description of what it means to be blessed and to live out of our true self in God rather than our identity in the world.

Blessed are the poor in spirit, for theirs is the kingdom of heaven.

Blessed are those who mourn, for they will be comforted.

Blessed are the meek, for they will inherit the earth.

Blessed are those who hunger and thirst for righteousness, for they will be filled.

Blessed are the merciful, for they will receive mercy.

Blessed are the pure in heart, for they will see God.

Blessed are the peacemakers, for they will be called the children of God.

Blessed are those that are persecuted for righteousness sake, for theirs is the kingdom of heaven.

Blessed are you when people revile you and persecute you and utter all kinds of evil against you falsely on my account. Rejoice and be glad, for your reward is great in heaven, for in the same way they persecuted the prophets who were before you.[175]

175.   Matthew 5:3-11.

The beatitudes are a perfect description of what we would look like if we identified with who we are in God rather than the person we are in the world. Those who identify with who they are in God have a spirit of poverty because they realize the illusion of the false-self and the lie of the happiness it pursues. The false-self is constantly trying to increase its stature in the world in order to appear to be more than their neighbor by increasing their wealth, power, prestige, talent, or beauty, but Jesus is constantly calling us to see such things as the fictions they are. The deeper life to which Jesus calls us is found in the poverty of being reduced to our true self or who we are in God.

> Blessed are the poor in spirit, for theirs is the kingdom of heaven.

Francis of Assisi is reported to have said, "I am who God says I am, no more and no less." That is the poverty and the giving away or dis-identifying with all of our possessions.[176] This is what brings us to our deeper life in God. When Jesus speaks to his disciples, he is always speaking to the deepest level of their being in God rather than their being in the world. At other times, however, when he speaks to the religious leaders of his day, he speaks to their false-self, which is the only self of which they are aware. The words that Jesus speaks to his disciples have to be heard from that deeper level of unitive consciousness that connects us to God and all other human beings. In prayer, at its deepest level of unitive consciousness, we are no longer aware of all those things that make us different from one another, but are only aware of that

---

176. Luke 14:33.

pure consciousness that we share with God and all other human beings. If we spend enough time in this pure consciousness of prayer, which gives us access to our deeper life in God, the words of Jesus make sense, in a way that they never do when we perceive them from the perspective of who we are in the world.

Of course, if we never spend time identifying with that deeper self that God created, we can all too easily imagine that God loves some false-selves and hates others. God, however, as "our Father" loves all of his creation, and we are all his daughters and sons. There is nothing we can do to increase God's love for us, but there is plenty we can do to increase our love for God and God's Creation. Loving God and all of his daughters and sons is its own reward. The love to which Jesus calls us is the experience of being set free from the false-self, which holds all of our judgments and unforgiveness. The false-self wants to be loved, but it has very little capacity to love. Its love is simply a response to having been loved, but it has little or no capacity to be the agents of God's love. The agents of God's love are those who are already passing into their angelic form through the death of the false-self.

Angelic beings operate out of who they are in God, rather than who they are in the world. They operate out of that unitive consciousness, which allows them to be more than isolated subjects surrounded by alien objects. From our unitive level of consciousness, we are no longer concerned with what we have to do to become the objects of love, but we are free to become the agents of God's love. From the unitive level of consciousness, we are able to see all human beings as our sisters and brothers, and are able to see the false-self for the illusion it is. This is the rich poverty which allows us to see and love our neighbor, and even our enemy, as ourselves.

That deeper self that we are in God has no possessions, since our possessions are the things that possess us and keep us tied to the false-self that we are in the world. Spiritual poverty is what sets us free to be who we are in God. It is not necessarily the same as economic poverty. As we have said, someone could give away all of their possessions and still identify with those possessions and the false-self that was able to acquire them. They can even take pride in being better than others for having done so. Indeed, the false-self can give away all of its possessions, in order for the false-self to try and find favor with God, but there is nothing we can do to find favor with God. God loves all of his children and there is nothing we can do to get God to love us anymore than God already does. We, however, can come to love God and God's creation more through our disidentification with the false-self.

Spiritual poverty is our detachment and disidentification from the world in order to participate in the reign of God. Jesus' life was completely surrendered to his Father's will, and he calls us into that same surrender in order to experience the fullness of life in God, which comes with the death of the false-self and our detachment from the world. This is what the great saints have always known, but it is the very thing that must be suppressed in order for Christian churches to grow in popularity.

The popular churches tell us that there is nothing wrong with being in the world. The Bible is all about God meeting us in our world and blessing us there. The popular churches claim that there is nothing new with Jesus and the Gospels, other than that Jesus is providing the ultimate remedy for our sin through the Cross. They claim that the good news is that we can have Jesus and the world as well, as long as we ignore the words of Jesus. The popular forms of Christianity have to suppress the words of Jesus because his words are constantly calling us to a radically different way to *be in God*, rather than the way the world has taught us to *be*.

> Blessed are those who mourn, for they will be comforted.

Mourning the passing of life, in order to enter more fully into life, is part of the great mystery that is beyond our understanding, but not beyond our experience. Furthermore, we do not have to wait until the end of life and our physical death in order to experience this mournful, transitional joy into the fullness of eternal life. This is what Jesus refers to when he tells us, "Those who love their life lose it, and those who hate their life in this world will keep it for eternal life."[177] This is one of the few sayings of Jesus that appears in all four of the Gospels. He says the same thing in the synoptic Gospels.

> For those who want to save their life will lose it, and those who lose their life for my sake will save it. What does it profit them if they gain the whole world, but lose or forfeit themselves?[178]

Some read this as referring to the many martyrs that would be a part of the early church, but it is also what every follower of Jesus will experience if they stay on the spiritual journey and come to identify with who they are in God rather than who they

---

177.   John 12:25.
178.   Luke 9:24-25; also see Matthew 10:39, 16:25; Mark 8:35.

are in the world. Spending time alone with God and Jesus' words are what produce the dying of the false-self in order that the reign of God might come forth in our life. How far we go on the spiritual journey to which Jesus calls us is largely a matter of how much dying we are willing to bear. Most Christians want Jesus to be their Savior in response to their right religious beliefs, but Jesus never speaks of our beliefs. Our beliefs have very little to do with who we actually are. As we have said, who we ultimately are is established by the things we love. Everyone professes to love Jesus, but they do not love the things he tells us to love. In fact, it is impossible to love the things he tells us to love from the perspective of who we are in the world. From our perspective in the world, no one loves their enemies. That requires the radically different perspective of who we are in God rather than who we are in the world. How much of Jesus' perspective we are able to make our own is largely determined by how much we are willing to mourn the death of the false-self. It is the false-self and all of its knowing that prevents us from hearing the words of Jesus and making those words our own. Our eternal life in God is established by how much or how little of Jesus' words have taken root at the core of our being. Who we are in the world is what prevents us from making Jesus' words our own, and the death of the false-self is what allows those words to take root in who we are in God.

If we identify with who we are in the world, we will identify with and love those possessions that make us better than other human beings. The false-self sees itself better than other human beings because of its wealth, power, talent, beauty, fame, or religious beliefs. That false-self can never love the way Jesus calls us to love, since the false-self imagines that God must love the way the false-self loves by discriminating between who is worthy of love and who is unworthy of love. But God is love and calls us to be love, without discrimination. In order for that to happen, the false-self, which sees my neighbor, and especially my enemy, as different from me, has to die. The world teaches us how to be more than others, while Jesus calls us in the opposite direction in order that we might find our littleness in God. The reign of God only comes forth in our life when we are out of the way. It is our littleness in God that allows the reign of God to come forth in our life. The word used to express that littleness in God is meekness.

> Blessed are the meek, for they will inherit the earth.[179]

Like all of the Beatitudes, this does not appear to be indicative of virtue. Indeed, it is the very antithesis of worldly virtue. In the world, we seek more of all the things that the world values and has to offer, but Jesus tells us that our godly virtue is found in our own littleness in order that the greatness of God might come forth in our lives. In order for God's mercy, forgiveness, and love to freely flow through us, there needs to be less and less of us in the way. I know we think of Jesus as powerful and moving in a confidence that made us see him as greater than other men, but that is not how he saw himself.

> Take my yoke upon you, and learn of me; for I am meek and lowly in heart: and ye shall find rest unto your souls. For my yoke is easy, and my burden is light."[180]

---

179.   Matthew 5:5.
180.   Matthew 11:29-30. KJV

Jesus' meekness comes from the fact that his identity is not in the world but in God. We might see him as great and powerful, and from our perspective in the world that appears to be true, but Jesus never identified with any of the world's virtues. He knew that he was God's beloved son – no more and no less. He knew that all of the accolades and treasures of the world are illusions that keep us from our true identity in God.

> Again, the devil took him to a very high mountain and showed him all the kingdoms of the world and their splendor; and he said to him, "All these I will give you, if you fall down and worship me." Jesus said to him, "Away with you Satan! for it is written, 'Worship the Lord your God, and serve him only.'"[181]

Jesus never succumbed to the temptations of the world, because he experienced being in God, rather than being in the world. Meekness is the virtue of preferring our littleness in God to our greatness in the world. Of course, in the world, no one desires meekness. You never hear kids telling other kids that when they grow up they want to be meek. That usually only comes with advanced spiritual growth, or more properly death, because we have experienced the folly of pursuing greatness in whatever form the world tells us to imagine it. We have trouble seeing Jesus as meek, because the world has made him into such an iconic figure, but if we seriously consider his life and his words, we see he is the epitome of meekness.

> Here is a man who was born in an obscure village, the child of a peasant woman. He grew up in another village. He worked

---

181.   Matthew 4:8-10.

in a carpenter shop until He was thirty. Then for three years He was an itinerant preacher. He never owned a home. He never wrote a book. He never held an office. He never had a family. He never went to college. He never put His foot inside a big city. He never traveled two hundred miles from the place He was born. He never did one of the things that usually accompany greatness.... While still a young man, the tide of popular opinion turned against him. His friends ran away. One of them denied Him. He was turned over to His enemies. He went through the mockery of a trial. He was nailed upon a Cross between two thieves. While He was dying His executioners gambled for the only piece of property He had on earth – His coat. When He was dead, He was laid in a borrowed grave through the pity of a friend. Twenty long centuries have come and gone, and today He is a centerpiece of the human race and leader of the column of progress. Of all the armies that ever marched, all the navies that were ever built; all the parliaments that ever sat and all the kings that ever reigned, put together, have not affected the life of man upon this earth as powerfully as has that one solitary life.[182]

Isn't it strange that although history recognizes the divine nature of a life so radically different from everything we imagine as blessed, most of us who consider ourselves his followers, and claim to love him, do not love the life he lived, and the life he calls us to live? The spiritual journey into the fullness of life leads us on a path into ever greater meekness. This is the divine wisdom

---

182.   This essay was adapted from a sermon by Dr. James Allan Francis in "The Real Jesus and Other Sermons" © 1926 by the Judson Press of Philadelphia (pp 123-124 titled "Arise Sir Knight!").

of Jesus: that blessedness is found in our meekness. The greatness of who Jesus was in God came out of the littleness of who he was in the world.

Our identity in the world is the great distraction that keeps us from our true identity in God. In the world, we strive to create an identity that distinguishes us from other human beings by being richer, more beautiful, more powerful, more talented, or more spiritual than other human beings; but our identity in God is indistinguishable from who other human beings are in God. Who we are in God at the core of our being is indistinguishable from who our enemy is in God at the core of their being. Jesus' teachings are about trying to get us back to who we were in God before the world got a hold of us and began making us into its likeness. This is why he tells us "You must be born from above"[183] or born again in order to discover who we were in God before the world got a hold of us and started making us in its likeness rather than the likeness of our Father. This is also why he tells us that,

> Unless you change and become like little children, you will never enter the kingdom of heaven. Therefore, whoever takes the lowly position of this child is the greatest in the kingdom of heaven.[184]

Jesus is always calling us to that deeper self of who we were in God before the world got a hold of us. Who we are in God is that original self that was completely cared for by another being. Of course, once we began to identify with who we were outside

---

183.　John 3:7.
184.　Matthew 18:3-4.

the womb, we increasingly became the acquisitive self that is always interested in acquire things to make us appear to be more than we are. We even want to acquire God's love, and religion is usually good at telling us how to do that, but God is love and there is nothing we can do to get God to love us any more than God already does. Following Jesus is not about getting God to love us more, but about getting us to love God and his Creation more.

Of course, the mind that connects us to the world rather than God is all about the false-self getting our needs met better than the false-selves of our neighbors getting their needs met. This is why Jesus is always attacking religion because it is the false-self's efforts to acquire God's love rather than being God's love to the world. The more loving we become, the more we resemble the Divine. What prevents us from becoming more loving is our attachment to the world and all of the things the world tells us we have to acquire in order to become happy. Worldly religion also tells us that we have to acquire God's love through our right beliefs or behavior. Tribal religion tells us that God does not love everyone but only people who believe and behave as my tribal religion prescribes. In contrast to tribal religion which tells us how to acquire what we need to be acceptable to God, Jesus tells us that we need to be meek in order to realize that God loves us because of who God is and not because of something special about us.

The virtue of meekness is most rare, since the world is always tempting us to be more, rather than less. This is what makes the Gospels so different from all of the scriptures that preceded them. The scriptures are the story of God meeting human beings in the world and blessing them there. When people initially encounter God they imagine that this God that they have encountered is strong and powerful like the rulers of this world. The rulers of this world are never meek and we have enormous trouble believing that the greatest of all rulers is meek and would rather suffer evil and destroy it with forgiveness rather than with power. This is the mystery of forgiveness that we refuse to embrace. We want a God that is more like us and less like Jesus, so we make up theologies that give us what we want, rather than embracing the mystery of the meekness of God. We want a God that defeats evil through power and strength rather than a God that transforms evil with forgiveness and love. That is the divine wisdom that is so hard to understand and why we much prefer those scriptures that present a more human perspective of God rather than the divine perspective that Jesus offers.

To defeat evil with forgiveness requires the virtue of meekness, but meekness is not high on our lists of the virtues that we wish to acquire. It usually takes a great deal of time and transformation before we can even see the beauty of Wesley's great line, "gentle Jesus, meek and mild." Once we start to understand meekness, however, we begin to see how different Jesus and the Gospels are from everything that came before them, and how different his kingdom is from the world.

> Blessed are those who hunger and thirst for righteousness, for
> they will be filled.[185]

Notice that the blessed are those who hunger and thirst for righteousness. Throughout the Gospels, we see Jesus constantly rebuking the religious leaders who consider themselves

---

185.   Matthew 5:6.

righteous. They saw themselves as righteous through their obedience to behavioral laws and their religious traditions and beliefs.
Jesus, however, tells us that righteousness is something to hunger and thirst after and not something to claim as a possession.
Christianity Lite tells us how to get our sins forgiven in order
to be righteous; Jesus tells us how to acquire the divine virtues
of forgiveness, mercy, and love because all of the law and the
prophets hang on the two commandments of loving God with
all of our heart, soul, and mind, and loving our neighbor as ourselves.[186] We all fall short of those two commandments and only
our constant repentance or changing our minds about our own
righteousness keeps us in the flow of God's transformative forgiveness and mercy.

From our perspective in the world, we think that right beliefs
and the avoidance of sin puts us in good stead with God; but if we
wish to follow Jesus into his kingdom, we begin to see that our
real sin is that we do not love God with all of our heart, soul, and
mind; and we do not love our neighbor as ourselves. In order to
love much, we must be forgiven much, since "the one to whom
little is forgiven, loves little."[187] This is why Jesus tells us that our
sin is deeper than we imagine and so is our need for repentance
and the ever-deeper experience of God's forgiveness and mercy.

Kingdom living is a life of repentance or changing our minds
about who we are in order to identify with who we are in God,
rather than who we are in the world. We may begin the life to
which Jesus calls us through repentance for our disobedience, but

---

186.   Matthew 22:36-40; Mark 12:28-31; Luke 10:27.
187.   Luke 7:47.

we proceed into a deeper identity in God and his kingdom through repentance over our lack of love, lack of forgiveness, and lack of mercy. The righteousness to which Jesus calls us is not a matter of becoming sinless, but a matter of becoming ever more awareness of our need for forgiveness and mercy on ever deeper levels in order that we might become God's forgiveness and mercy to the world, for having received much forgiveness and mercy.

Blessed are the merciful for they will receive mercy.[188]

Later in the Sermon on the Mount, Jesus tells us that God does not judge us at all but allows us to judge ourselves by the way we judge others. "Do not judge, so that you may not be judged. For with the judgment you make you will be judged, and the measure you give will be the measure you get."[189] Mercy, in a sense, is the opposite of justice in that justice is getting what we deserve, while mercy is not getting what we deserve. The more we extend mercy to others, the more merciful we become. Mercy, like forgiveness and love, increases the more we give it away. "Go and learn what this means, 'I desire mercy, not sacrifice.' For I have come to call not the righteous but sinners."[190]

Our ability to extend mercy to others is dependent upon our ability to receive mercy. The righteous have no access to mercy, but desire justice for both themselves and others. This was the central problem that Jesus had with the religious people of his day, and it is still a problem with most religious people. They desire a

---

188.   Matthew 5:7.
189.   Matthew 7:1-3.
190.   Luke Matthew 9:13; also 12:7.

just God who gives people what they deserve in terms of reward or punishment, but according to Jesus' teachings the only reward is our becoming more like our heavenly Father in terms of mercy, forgiveness, and love. Those are the virtues that allow us to be free in God.

Justice, as getting what we deserve, is a very human and worldly concept. In the world, justice is what allows us to claim things as our own, but in God nothing is our own. Only the false-self or who we are in the world has possessions. In David Hume's, *An Enquiry Concerning the Principles of Morals*, he says that in heaven every virtue would flourish except justice or respect for what is one's own.

> It seems evident, that, in such a happy state, every other social virtue would flourish, and receive tenfold increase; but the cautious, jealous virtue of justice, would never once have been dreamt of. For what purpose make a partition of goods, where everyone has already more than enough?[191]

Hume's point is that in both circumstances of great abundance and great privation, property rights are non-existent. When there is great abundance, if someone should take the apple from your hand, you simply pick another apple. Likewise, when there is great scarcity, the fact that the apple is in your hand does not stop another from taking it from you in order to survive. There is no justice in either heaven or hell. It is only in this middle realm between heaven and hell where justice is a virtue. Even Aristotle knew that when

---

191.   Hume, David. *An Inquiry concerning the Principles of Morals*. Ed. Ralph Cohen. *The Essential Works of David Hume*. New York: Bantam Books, 1965, p. 190.

human beings function out of that deeper level of consciousness where we recognize our connection to God and other human beings, there is no need for justice. He says, "When men are friends, they have no need of justice at all."[192] Justice certainly has a place, but it is a worldly place rather than a heavenly place.

Blessed are the pure in heart, for they will see God.[193]

God is omnipresent, but we are constantly distracted from an awareness of the Divine presence by all those things that so easily capture and demand our attention. A pure heart is the essential condition for the kind of prayer that Jesus understood and practiced. It is also what it means to love God, as Jesus says, with all of our heart, soul, and mind.[194] In our normal state of being in the world, our hearts and minds are distracted from an awareness of God's divine presence by what Jesus will tell us are our real sins, which are all those things which attach us to the world and keep us from experiencing that pure heart that is capable of focusing on God alone, rather than the distractions of the world.

In order to realize this beatitude of being able to see God, we have to be able to get to that place of a pure heart where our attention is no longer distracted by the things of the world, and we experience nothing but the silence and stillness of God's presence. Only silence and stillness are big enough to contain the experience of God's presence. Words and images are the illusions of the false-self. The way we know that the silence and stillness

---

192.   Aristotle. *Nicomachean Ethics*. VIII. 1. 27.

193.   Matthew 5:8.

194.   Matthew 22:37. Also Deuteronomy 6:5; Mark 12:30; and Luke 10:27.

192 JESUS AND THE BICAMERAL BRAIN

of our soul represents the experience of God's presence is that when we are in that silent and still place, we can see the beauty and goodness of Jesus words. As we have said, it is impossible to hear Jesus' words from the perspective of who we are in the world. If we live out of the mind the world has given us, we will always ignore the words of Jesus and create religious doctrines that find ways around them.

Of course, most people's idea of prayer has little to do with experiencing God's presence in order to hear the words of Jesus. Most people pray out of the left-brain's understanding that the world has given us. From that perspective, they can believe that God is listening, but Jesus tells us that God is not only listening but "your Father knows what you need before you ask him."[195] If our Father knows what we need before we ask, what is the point of asking or using words in general? Prayer is not about making requests of God or offering thanksgiving to God. Prayer is the place we go in order to establish an identity in God that is different from our identity in the world, because it is only from the perspective of who we are in God, rather than who we are in the world, that we can hear the words of Jesus.

Prayer is the practice of that pure heart that is not distracted by the world and the constant flow of data to which the world constantly demands we pay attention. Purity of heart is that alternative level of consciousness that is prayer as Jesus understood it. Our hearts, souls, and minds are constantly distracted and occupied by the things of the world. Prayer is what silences all those voices in order to become aware of God's indwelling presence. This is not

---

195.   Matthew 6:8.

part of our left-brain's knowing but the pure and silent awareness that opens us to the beauty and goodness of Jesus' words.

> Blessed are the peacemakers, for they will be called children of God.[196]

Peacemakers are those who are always willing to stand in the middle between two warring groups and not take sides but allow themselves to be the bridge which both sides will trample upon. Jesus' followers are called to be peacemakers because they love both sides in whatever conflict arises. When we are in the world, we take sides; but when we are in God, there is only God's side. God sees both sides as wrong and in need of repentance for not loving their neighbor as themselves. This is what the peacemaker sees as well.

Indeed, all of the Beatitudes are about seeing things from Jesus' divine perspective rather than from the perspective the world has given us. In the world, we operate out of what our left-brain claims to know. Jesus, however, is constantly calling us to the pure awareness of our being in God, rather than our *being right* because of what we know and believe. Only love counts with God, and that extends to both sides in every conflict. The next two Beatitudes or blessings follow along this same line as that of the peacemaker.

> Blessed are those who are persecuted for righteousness' sake, for theirs is the kingdom of heaven.

> Blessed are you when people revile you and persecute you and utter all kinds of evil against you falsely on my account. Rejoice and be glad, for your reward is great in heaven, for in

---

196.   Matthew 5:9.

the same way they persecuted the prophets who were before you.[197]

These are not the kinds of things we consider blessings from the perspective of who we are in the world. We should also note that these are the kinds of blessings that the Jewish prophets understood as they brought correction to the religious and secular authorities of their day. It is interesting to note at this point that in addition to everything else, Jesus is the last of the great Jewish prophets and is calling his followers to that same tradition of standing out and apart from the world in order to shed a heavenly light upon the world. Jesus' words seldom tell us what to know or believe, but rather how to love and how to be in God rather than in the world.

We have created a religion in Jesus' name and forged religious beliefs in order to make that religion compatible and attractive to our existence in the world. In order to do so, however, we needed to find ways around Jesus' teachings, since Jesus' words are simply too counter-cultural to be taken seriously by people who identify with who they are in the world. Saints may pay attention to Jesus' words, but most who consider themselves Christians avoid them like the plague. The popular forms of Christianity create doctrines and theologies from a great variety of scriptures in order to show us how to be righteous before God through our beliefs and religious behavior, just as the religious people in Jesus' day did. Jesus' words, however, are always calling us to something deeper.

Jesus is always speaking about an entirely different way to be, than the way the world has taught us to be. It is a detached

197.   Matthew 5:10-12.

existence that is free from the world; it is a rich poverty that recognizes the illusions to which the false-self so easily attaches itself. It is an existence that mourns the death of the false-self, and seeks meekness in order to make room for the divine virtues of mercy and forgiveness. This is the purity of heart to which he calls us, and the only real source of peace. Jesus ends the beatitudes by telling us that such a life will put us at enmity with the world, but being at enmity with the world, because we no longer identify with its values, is the only way to hear the words of Jesus. If we do not have a daily practice of going to that place of detachment from the world, where we can be alone with God and apart from the world, we will drift back into the world and live according to its ways rather than according to Jesus' words.

You may have a religious conviction that you are saved by your belief that Jesus' death was payment for your sins, but you are entering eternal life as the person that the world created rather than the person that Jesus' words are intended to create. You may like the way your wealth, power, and prestige makes you look in the eyes of other human beings, but that only has a negative effect upon your eternal life in God, which is not established by how much love you have received from the world, but how much love you have given to the world. That is what the great saints of every tradition have always understood.

Christianity Lite claims that our right religious beliefs change the heart of God toward us from one of wrath to one of love. But God loves all of his creation, and calls us to love all of his creation as well. Of course, the world has taught us to love those parts of God's creation that look and think as we do. Love, however, is bigger than our understanding, but we cannot see that from the perspective that the world has given us. In the world, we see love through the perspective the world has given us, but Jesus offers us a perspective from which to see as God sees. God has given us the enormous freedom to create our own eternal nature by how much or how little of Jesus' perspective we choose to make our own.

CHAPTER TEN

The Gospel

God is perfectly merciful and loves without restriction, but we can only see that when we can get to a place from which we ourselves can love without restrictions. We can only see as much of God as our perspective allows. Thus, there is a huge gap between God and our understanding of God. Of course, many people believe that their understanding of God and the reality of who God actually is are identical. That is the problem with knowing and what prevents us from hearing Jesus' words. As we have repeatedly said, the mystery of God is always beyond our knowing but not beyond our experience. If we claim to know God, however, there is no need for further experiences that take us beyond what we know. Jesus' words are always calling us beyond what we know in order to reveal more of the mystery that is God and our relationship with God. Not knowing is what keeps us on the spiritual journey into the deeper truths of Jesus' words.

Jesus is offering us a perspective that is radically different from the perspective we have inherited from the world. Jesus' words reveal who we are in God rather than who we are in the world. In order to receive his words, we have to detach from the world and the understanding the world has given us—especially the understanding the world has given us concerning God and our relationship with God.

People love the Bible because it speaks to where they are at. We ignore the words of Jesus because they do not speak to where we are at, but where God is calling us to be. If you think that Jesus' words and the Bible are saying the same thing, you are not paying attention to Jesus' words. Jesus tells us that God does not judge us but gives us the freedom to create our own eternal nature by the things we choose to love. Jesus' words tell us the best things to love in order that our eternal nature will be more like the Divine rather than the world. How much or how little we heed Jesus' words is what shapes our eternal being.

> I do not judge anyone who hears my words and does not keep them, for I came not to judge the world, but to save the world. The one who rejects me and does not receive my word has a judge; on the last day the word that I have spoken will serve as judge, for I have not spoken on my own, but the Father who sent me has himself given me a commandment about what to say and what to speak. And I know that his commandment is eternal life. What I speak, therefore, I speak just as the Father has told me."[198]

Jesus says that the words he has spoken will be our judge. His words tell us what we should love, in order to love as our heaven Father loves. Of course, the world also has a lot to say about what and how we should love as well. The nature of the spiritual journey to which Jesus calls us is about falling in love with Jesus

---

198.   John 12:47-50.

words and making them the foundation for our eternal being. In order to do that, we need that larger, unitive consciousness that experiences our connection to God and all other human beings. Without that unitive consciousness that we are able to experience in prayer, God will be seen as an object to be worshipped and obeyed rather than as "our Father" who desires his daughters and sons to take on his divine nature and love.

What Jesus taught his disciples was how to live out of being in God rather than being in the world. His teachings represent a life that was lived out of that perspective, but everyone has to find that perspective of being in God on their own – it is radically unique to our personal relationship with God. The more time we spend alone with God, the more the Holy Spirit is able to explain Jesus' words to us.

> I have said these things to you while I am still with you. But the Advocate, the Holy Spirit, whom the Father will send in my name, will teach you everything, and remind you of all that I have said to you.[199]

The role of the Holy Spirit, which is God's indwelling presence, is to remind us of all that Jesus has said.

> Those who love me will keep my word, and my Father will love them, and we will come to them and make our home with them. Whoever does not love me does not keep my words; and the word that you hear is not mine, but is from the Father who sent me.[200]

---

199.   John 14:26.
200.   John 14:23-24.

Jesus taught his disciples to pray as he prayed; that is, in order to hear God's words, just as Jesus heard them. As we have seen, that requires a different perspective and a different level of consciousness than the one the world has given us. Throughout the Bible, we have story after story of how God revealed himself to people in the world and how they understood those experiences from their perspective in the world. Jesus, however, tells us how to experience God from the perspective and level of consciousness of our being in God rather than being in the world.

> And when you pray, you are not to be like the hypocrites; for they love to stand and pray in the synagogues and on the street corners so that they will be seen by people. Truly I say to you, they have their reward in full. But as for you, when you pray, go into your inner room, close your door, and pray to your Father who is in secret; and your Father who sees what is done in secret will reward you.
>
> And when you are praying, do not use thoughtless repetition as the Gentiles do, for they think that they will be heard because of their many words. So do not be like them; for your Father knows what you need before you ask Him.[201]

Prayer, as the world has taught us to pray, is very different from how Jesus teaches us to pray. Jesus is trying to teach us how to hear from God by detaching ourselves from the world. The inner room with the shut door is Jesus' metaphor for that other level of consciousness where we are apart from the world and the understanding that the world has given us. Prayer, as Jesus

---

201.   Matthew 6:5-8. NASV

understood it, is that unitive level of consciousness where Jesus experienced his oneness with his Father and our Father. This is the deep state of prayer, where we are no longer subjects perceiving a world of objects, but are immersed in God. When we experience our being in God and God being in us, we understand our intimate and familial connection to God, as our Father, and all other human beings as sisters and brothers. This is not the understanding and perspective the world has given us.

The understanding which the left-brain provides gives us the knowledge we need to survive and prosper in the world. The words of Jesus are never compatible with that understanding. Jesus' words only make sense from the perspective of who we are in God at the core of our being. The false-self that we project to the world, is deaf to Jesus' words. If we never go to that inner room and shut the door in order to discover who we are in God, we will never hear the words of Jesus and never experience the richness of life that comes from making his words our own. God has given us the enormous freedom to create our own eternal nature by the things we choose to love. Jesus does not tell us what to believe but what to love in order to create ourselves in the likeness of the Divine rather than the likeness of the world.

Jesus is always turning the world upside down and telling us that the rich and powerful are cursed and the poor and meek are blessed. That is because the truth of our being is not determined by the world and its values, but by the fact that we are the daughters and sons of the most-high God, who Jesus refers to as *our Father*. What keeps us from that identity in God is our identity in the world. If we never go to that deep place of prayer where we identify with God rather than the world, we will never take Jesus' words seriously and will always find ways around them in order to feel righteous rather than repentant.

The bicameral brains allows us to see both the intricate details in things and what makes one thing different from another, but it also allows us to see the connections between things. We have recently discovered that the roots of trees are not merely connected to the ground but also to one another. The human brain, likewise, is not only capable of understanding the details that make things different from one another, but also how things are connected to one another. All of Jesus' teachings are about getting us to see those connections in order that we might love our neighbor, and even our enemy, as ourselves. Unfortunately, the modern world has taught us to think almost exclusively out of the subject/object distinction of the left-brain. As left-brain thinkers, the form of Christianity that most find attractive focuses upon the personal salvation of the individual through a faith in Jesus as payment for our sins. Our personal salvation through our religious beliefs resonates with our left-brain, but Jesus only addresses that level of consciousness when he is speaking to the religious leaders of his day. When he speaks to his disciples, he speaks to who they are in God, since it is only who we are in God that desires to love our enemy or to give without expecting to receive. Only who we are in God can refuse to respond to violence with violence, and only who we are in God can judge no one and forgive everyone.

Jesus did not preach salvation through the forgiveness of sins in response to our religious beliefs, although that is where most Christians begin the spiritual journey. Jesus calls us to become God's forgiveness and mercy to the world. That makes no sense to the understanding the world has given us. It only makes sense to who Jesus is calling us to be, and that only makes sense from that deeper level of unitive consciousness that we are able to experience in prayer. The way we get to that deeper level of consciousness is through repentance or changing our minds about who we are. Without repentance or changing our mind about who we are, we will never take the teachings of Jesus seriously. As long as we identify with who we are in the world, we will always prefer a gospel that is something to believe rather than something to become. Jesus' words, however, are always about our being rather than our beliefs. How much or how little of his word has taken root at the core of our being is what creates the nature of our eternal being. It is not what we believe that determines our eternal nature but what we love, and Jesus' teachings tell us the best things to love in order to create an eternal existence that looks more like our heavenly Father than the world. We will share eternity with beings that love what we love, so choose wisely by paying attention to Jesus' words.

The spiritual journey that is the gospel, like the Bible itself, is a transformative journey. We begin with a God who resembles human authorities that demand obedience and punish disobedience, but Jesus tells us that God is our Father whose only desire is that his daughters and sons would become like him in terms of character and virtue. God is love and we have been made in his image with love at the core of our being. We have also been made free, however, and are able to direct that love as we choose. Our love is what attaches us to those things from which we hope to find happiness and meaning for our lives. Jesus' words point us toward the best things to love, but we can only see how good and beautiful those things are from the perspective of who we are in God, rather than who we are in the world.

Jesus' words are always calling us to a deeper life than the life we have in the world. In order to get to that deeper life, we have to respond to Jesus' words with repentance or changing our minds from how the world has taught us to be, to how Jesus is calling us to be. From our perspective in the world, we simply want our sins to be forgiven, but from the perspective to which Jesus calls us, we are able to see our sin at ever deeper levels. From our perspective in the world, sin is what alienates us from God; from Jesus' perspective sin is what keeps us from the fullness of life in God. Sin, at its deepest level, is that we identify with who we are in the world rather than who we are in God. We want our sins to be the sins that the world recognizes, and not our lack of love. We do not want to see our failures to forgive everyone,[202] and judge no one[203] as sin. That is further down the line than we want to go. We want Jesus to simply take away our sins so we might see ourselves as righteous, but righteousness is part of the illusion of the false-self or who we want to be in the eyes of the world.

> The Pharisees, who were lovers of money, heard all this, and they ridiculed him. So he said to them, "You are those who justify yourself in the sight of others; but God knows your hearts; for what is prized by human beings is an abomination in the sight of God.[204]

---

202.   Matthew 6:15, and Mark 11:26.
203.   Matthew 7:1-2.
204.   Luke 16:15.

And Jesus' brother, James echoes those same words.

> Adulterers! Do you not know that friendship with the world
> is enmity with God? Therefore whoever wishes to be a friend
> of the world becomes an enemy of God.[205]

This is sin at its deepest level; that is, that we identify with who the world tells us to be rather than who Jesus tells us to be. We claim to want his kingdom, but we want it to look like the world. If we paid attention to his words, however, we would see that his kingdom is nothing like the world, and who Jesus is calling us to be is nothing like the person that we are in the world. We want our sins to be covered by Jesus' forgiveness and mercy, but Jesus wants us to become his forgiveness and mercy to the world. As we have said, receiving forgiveness and mercy is for the purpose of making us forgiving and merciful, and not for the purpose of making us righteous in the sense of being sinless. Being sinless is the world's notion of righteousness. Jesus' notion of righteousness results from seeing our sin at ever deeper levels in order that God's mercy and forgiveness might continue to flow through us in order to transform us into his merciful and forgiving likeness.

From our perspective in the world, we want our righteousness to be a matter of being sinless, but that is not the kind of righteousness that Jesus is talking about. Jesus' words are calling us to become his forgiveness and mercy to the world. That only happens by us seeing our sin at ever deeper levels in order that his forgiveness and mercy continues to flow through us. It is Leonard Cohen's beautiful line, "There is a crack in everything (there is a

---

205.   Also see James 4:4.

crack in everything). That's how the light gets in." Popular religion tries to fix the cracks in order to make us appear righteous in the eyes of the world, but Jesus' words are always revealing deeper cracks that will let in the light of God's forgiveness and mercy.

The repentance to which Jesus calls us to is not repentance for this or that particular sin, but repentance or changing our minds about who we are. We are not who we purport to be in the world. That is the false-self that we and the world have created. We are God's beloved daughters and sons, but we have to daily choose to live out of that identity rather than the identity the world has given us. This repentance, or changing of our mind, is a lifelong process of dying to who the world has made us to be in order for our life in God to come forth. That does not happen with a new belief, although it may, and usually does, begin there.

Jesus' teachings represent the ultimate truth of who God made us to be. The more we build our life upon his words, the closer we come to the ultimate truth of our being. As we have seen, the truth of the gospel is something to be and not something to merely claim to know and believe. The gospel is about our being in God rather than our being in the world, and our being *in* God only comes about through the death of who we are in the world.

> For those who want to save their life will lose it, and those who lose their life for my sake will find it. For what will it profit them if they gain the whole world but forfeit their life?[206]

---

206.   Matthew 16:25-26.

Following Jesus is all about the death of the false-self in order that we might come into the fullness of life in God. This death, however, is not something we can do, but something that God does with our permission. This is the ultimate form of prayer whereby we enter into God's presence and give God permission to detach us from those things which keep us from the fullness of life in God. Of course, God has made us free and we get to decide how far we want to go with God. How much time do we want to spend in God's presence in order to understand the words of Jesus? We all get to decide how much or how little of Jesus' words we are willing to make our own.

As we have seen, the nature of our bicameral brain gives us access to different levels of consciousness and different perspectives. We have both a calculating mind and a contemplative mind available for our use. One part of our brain connects us to the world and all we need to know to survive and flourish in this world, and the other part connects us to those deeper levels of our being which extends beyond this world. Unfortunately, both the science and religion of modern culture has become dominated by the calculating mind which tells us what we need to know, rather than how we need to be.

Life is not about knowing God, which is always beyond us. In fact, as we have said, when someone says they know God that is another way of saying they have gone far enough with God, and do not want to go any further for fear of losing the self that they have created to be in the world. Knowing, or our pretense to knowing, is what connects us to the world. The apophatic experience of not knowing is what opens us to the transformative experience of Jesus' words.

Certainly, most of us begin the spiritual journey on the epistemic level by believing the maps and doctrines that our culture provides concerning the gospel, but if we stay on the spiritual journey and have a practice of spending time in God's presence and Jesus' words, we are brought eventually to that deeper reality of the gospel, not as a belief, but as the ultimate truth of our being. How far we wish to go into that truth is what determines the nature and character of our eternal being. The gospel is something to become as more and more of Jesus' words take root within us.

On the left-brain's level of epistemic religious beliefs, religions vary enormously; but on the unitive level of consciousness that we are able to experience in prayer, the beauty and goodness of Jesus' words can be seen by people of all religions. Mohandas Gandhi (1869-1948) was not a Christian, but he had a prayer practice which allowed him to see the divine words of the Sermon on the Mount, which he claimed were true, even if Jesus had never existed. Our left-brain is what divides us into warring tribes, but our right-brain gives us access to that unitive consciousness that is the basis for all of morality and spirituality. The beauty and goodness of Jesus' words can only be seen from that unitive level of consciousness.

Human beings are certainly double-minded with one mind being attached to the world and all we need to know in order to be in the world, and another mind that connects us to God and all other human beings. If our lives are directed by the inherited understanding that most of us have received from the world, we will opt for religious beliefs that promise forgiveness in response to those beliefs, but always fall short of making us into the forgiving and merciful creatures Jesus calls us to be. The false-self is capable of believing that it has been forgiven, but it cannot be God's forgiveness to the world. The false-self can only be the object of love and not its agent. In order to be God's love to the world, we have to identify with who we are in God rather than who we are in the world.

From the perspective the world has given us, and out of which we create the false-self, we can act morally and religiously for fear of punishment, from either other people or God, but it will always be an act in the interests of the false-self, which hopes to find favor with our fellow human beings or God. Jesus does sometimes address the false-self, especially the false-selves of the religious leaders of his day, but when addressing his disciples, he is speaking to who they are in God rather than the person they are in the world. That is why prayer, or getting alone with God in order to discover who we were in God before the world got a hold of us, is so important. As we have said, that is the only perspective that allows us to see the beauty and goodness of Jesus' words. We know we are in God's presence when we are able to see how beautiful it is to forgive everyone, judge no one, and love even your enemies.

Again, we will spend eternity with beings who love what we love, so choose wisely. Jesus' words tell us the best things to love in order that our eternal existence might be heavenly rather than hellish. People in hell love the wealth, power, and prestige they eternal fight over. The desire to be more rather than less is what makes it hell, and being reduced to nothing but love is what makes it heaven. The world tells us our possessions add to what and who we are, but Jesus calls us to be free from all those things that possess us and keep us from the fullness of life in God. Our attachments to the world are what keep us from the fullness of life in God, and our detachment from the world is what allows us to hear the words of Jesus.

The false-self that we have created to be in the world can never love our neighbor as ourselves because our neighbor is nothing like the false-self that we have created to be in the world. We love the false-self because it is our creation rather than God's. I can only love my neighbor as myself when I recognize us both as God's creation rather than our own creation. That is the level of consciousness and perspective we have to get back to in order in order to hear the gospel, not as something to believe but something to become as Jesus' words continue to take root within us.

The gospel is not a theological belief that promises to save us from hell, but the body of Jesus' teachings which are meant to make us into his likeness. In order for that to happen, we have to see the gospel as a being thing rather than a knowing thing. We grow into the gospel as more and more of Jesus' words take root within us. Jesus' words are the "rock of ages" upon which God desires that we would form the nature and character of our eternal being, but those words can never take root in the false-self that we have created in order to be in the world. They require the deep soil of our soul, or who we are in God, rather than who the world has made us to be. This is the deep repentance that involves the death of the false-self. In order to enter into that deeper life in God, our life and identity in the world has to end.

> If any want to become my followers, let them deny them-
> selves and take up their cross daily and follow me. For those

who want to save their life will lose it, and those who lose their life for my sake will save it. What does it profit them if they gain the whole world, but lose or forfeit themselves? Those who are ashamed of me and of my words, of them the Son of Man will be ashamed....[207]

We love the Bible, because it speaks to where we are at in the world. We hate the words of Jesus, because they tell us that we have to die in order for God's life to come forth within us. We want to believe that we are in a good place with God, but Jesus is always calling us to a better place, if we can hear his words. Claiming to know God is what keeps us from that better place. As we have said, claiming to know God is another way of saying we have gone far enough with God, and we do not want to go any further for fear of losing the self that we have created. We love the self that we have created and only time alone with God and Jesus' words can prepare us for its death and the fullness of life that comes as we identify with who we are in God rather than the person we have created to be in the world.

The person we created to be in the world desires to be greater than our sisters and brothers, and popular religions appeal to that desire of the false-self, but we can never love our neighbor as ourselves from that perspective. From the perspective of Christianity Lite there are the saved and unsaved, but from God's perspective we are all his daughters and sons. The popular religions tell us what we have to believe and add to our existence in order to be pleasing to God, but the Gospels tell us that we must decrease in

---

207.   Luke 9:23-26. Also see, Matthew 10:38-39, 16:24-26; Mark 8:34-36; and Luke 14:27.

order for our Father's likeness to increase within us. The gospel is about growth through subtraction or more properly through death. The more the false-self dies, the more our life in God comes forth. When God is a distant sovereign who desires obedience and punishes disobedience, we seek to be righteous in the form of being sinless, but when God is "our Father" we seek to be like him in character and virtue.

This life is merely a birth canal into eternal life, but it is a very unique birth canal through which we get to choose the nature and character of our eternal being by the things we choose to love. Jesus' words tell us the best things to love in order that our eternal existence would resemble the Divine rather than the world. God loves the souls in hell as much as he loves the souls in heaven, but the souls in heaven get to love God more. That is the great reward of heaven. Life is eternal and so is the gospel. How much or how little of Jesus' words have taken root within us is what determines where we enter eternity, but the gospel of Jesus' words will eternally draw us into the fullness of life in God.